TREE HOMES

Teacher's Guide

Preschool–1

Skills

Observing, Describing, Comparing, Matching,
Sorting and Classifying, Communicating,
Creative- and Logical-Thinking,
Math Reasoning, Problem Solving

Concepts

Animal Shelter, Habitat, Measurement,
Parenting, Heat and Warmth, Friction,
Size and Shape, Tree Structure,
Animal Features and Behaviors

Themes

Patterns of Change, Stability, Scale, Structure,
Energy, Systems and Interactions,
Diversity and Unity

_Phoenixzoo.org/zoo/
animal/facts/racoon
– loomcam.com/raccoons

Hou

Math Strands

Measurement, Number, Logic and Language

by

Jean C. Echols and Jaine Kopp

with

Ellen Blinderman and Kimi Hosoume

LHS GEMS

GEMS
Great Explorations in Math and Science
Lawrence Hall of Science
University of California at Berkeley

Lawrence Hall of Science
University of California
Berkeley, CA 94720

Chairman: Glenn T. Seaborg
Director: Marian C. Diamond

Development of this guide was sponsored in part by a grant from the National Science Foundation.

Initial support for the origination and publication of the GEMS series was provided by the A.W. Mellon Foundation and the Carnegie Corporation of New York. GEMS has also received support from the McDonnell-Douglas Foundation and the McDonnell-Douglas Employees Community Fund, the Hewlett Packard Company Foundation, and the people at Chevron USA. GEMS also gratefully acknowledges the contribution of word processing equipment from Apple Computer, Inc. This support does not imply responsibility for statements or views expressed in publications of the GEMS program.

Under a grant from the National Science Foundation, GEMS Leader's Workshops have been held across the country. For further information on GEMS leadership opportunities, or to receive a publication brochure and the *GEMS Network News*, please contact GEMS at the address and phone number below.

COMMENTS WELCOME

Great Explorations in Math and Science (GEMS) is an ongoing curriculum development project. GEMS guides are revised periodically, to incorporate teacher comments and new approaches. We welcome your criticisms, suggestions, helpful hints, and any anecdotes about your experience presenting GEMS activities. Your suggestions will be reviewed each time a GEMS guide is revised. Please send your comments to:

GEMS Revisions
Lawrence Hall of Science
University of California, Berkeley, CA 94720.

Our phone number is (510) 642-7771.

STAFF

Principal Investigator
Glenn T. Seaborg
Director
Jacqueline Barber
Assistant Director
Kimi Hosoume
Curriculum Specialist
Cary Sneider
Staff Development Specialists
Katharine Barrett, John Erickson, Jaine Kopp, Laura Lowell, Linda Lipner, Laura Tucker, Carolyn Willard
Mathematics Consultant
Jan M. Goodman
Administrative Coordinator
Cynthia Eaton
Distribution Coordinator
Karen Milligan
Art Director
Lisa Haderlie Baker
Designers
Carol Bevilacqua and Lisa Klofkorn
Principal Editor
Lincoln Bergman
Senior Editor
Carl Babcock
Staff Assistants
Nancy Kedzierski, Felicia Roston, Vivian Tong, Stephanie Van Meter

Great Explorations in Math and Science (GEMS) Program

The Lawrence Hall of Science (LHS) is a public science center on the University of California at Berkeley campus. LHS offers a full program of activities for the public, including workshops and classes, exhibits, films, lectures, and special events. LHS is also a center for teacher education and curriculum research and development.

Over the years, LHS staff have developed a multitude of activities, assembly programs, classes, and interactive exhibits. These programs have proven to be successful at the Hall and should be useful to schools, other science centers, museums, and community groups. A number of these guided-discovery activities have been published under the Great Explorations in Math and Science (GEMS) title, after an extensive refinement process that includes classroom testing of trial versions, modifications to ensure the use of easy-to-obtain materials, and carefully written and edited step-by-step instructions and background information to allow presentation by teachers without special background in mathematics or science.

Contributing GEMS/PEACHES Authors

Jacqueline Barber
Katharine Barrett
Lincoln Bergman
Ellen Blinderman
Beatrice Boffen
Celia Cuomo
Linda De Lucchi
Jean Echols
John Erickson
Jaine Kopp
Jan M. Goodman
Alan Gould
Kimi Hosoume
Sue Jagoda
Linda Lipner
Laura Lowell
Larry Malone
Cary I. Sneider
Debra Sutter
Jennifer Meux White
Carolyn Willard

ACKNOWLEDGMENTS

Photographs: Richard Hoyt
Cover: Lisa Haderlie Baker
Illustrations: Rose Craig

Thanks to all the enthusiastic people on the PEACHES committee at the Lawrence Hall of Science—Katharine Barrett, Ellen Blinderman, Beatrice Boffen, Jean Echols, Tim Erickson, Kay Fairwell, Kimi Hosoume, Jaine Kopp, Bernadette Lauraya, Jennifer Meux White—for their many suggestions and other contributions during the development and writing of *Tree Homes*. A grateful note of appreciation goes to **Jaine Kopp**, who wrote the session on Sorting Bears.

We want to especially thank teachers **Linda Rogers** and **Kathy Hagerty** of the Brookfield Elementary School in Oakland, California for the generous gift of their time in helping us photograph the *Tree Homes* activities. And thanks go to the children in their kindergarten classes who graced the photographs in this guide.

REVIEWERS

We would like to thank the following educators who reviewed, tested, or coordinated the reviewing of *this series* of GEMS/PEACHES materials in manuscript and draft form. Their critical comments and recommendations, based on presentation of these activities nationwide, contributed significantly to these GEMS publications.

Their participation in the review process does not necessarily imply endorsement of the GEMS program or responsibility for statements or views expressed. Their role is an invaluable one, and their feedback is carefully recorded and integrated as appropriate into the publications.

ALASKA
Coordinator:
Cynthia Dolmas Curran

Iditarod Elementary School, Wasilla
Cynthia Dolmas Curran
Christina M. Jencks
Beverly McPeek
Abby Kellner-Rode

CALIFORNIA

GEMS Center, Huntington Beach
Coordinator: **Susan Spoeneman**

College View School,
Huntington Beach
Susan Gonzales
Anita Mueller
Elaine Ohgi
Sandra Silverman
Sandra Williamson

Francis Parker School, San Diego
Alyce Lynn

Haycox Elementary School, Oxnard
Margery Ann Leffingwell

Montessori Children Center,
Huntington Beach
Erin Karal
LeeAnne Clokey
Ellen Goodman

Solana Beach Child Development Center,
Solana Beach
Stacy Bermingham

Silverman Preschool, San Diego
Vicki Martin

Simi Valley Adult School, Simi Valley
Irene Garcia

Tierra Vista, Oxnard
Helen Faul

Town and Country Nursery School,
Palos Verdes
Raye Murphy

Trinity Lutheran Preschool, Simi Valley
Jenny Kidd

SAN FRANCISCO BAY AREA
Coordinators: **Cynthia Ashley**
Cynthia Eaton

4C's Children's Center, Oakland
Yolanda Coleman-Wilson

24 Hour Children Center, Oakland
Sheryl Lambert
Ella Tassin
Inez Watson

Afterschool Program, Piedmont
Willy Chen

Alameda Head Start, Alameda
Debbie Garcia
Stephanie Josey
Michelle Garabedian

Albany Children's Center, Albany
Celestine Whittaker

Bancroft School, Berkeley
Cecilia Saffarian

Bartell Childcare and Learning Center,
Oakland
Beverly Barrow
Barbara Terrell

Beach Elementary School, Piedmont
Ann Blasius
Juanita Forester
Jean Martin
Elodee Lessley

Belle Vista Child Development Center,
Oakland
Satinder Jit K. Rana

Berkeley Head Start, Berkeley
Marian Simmons
Alma Johnson
Xotchilt Del Carmen
Robinson
Rose Mary Wagner

Berkeley Hills Nursery School, Berkeley
Elizabeth Fulton

Berkeley-Albany YMCA, Berkeley
Trinidad Caselis

Berkeley/Richmond Jewish
Community, Berkeley
Terry Amgott-Kwan

Bernice & Joe Play School, Oakland
Bernice Huisman-Humbert

Bing School, Stanford
Kate Ashbey

Butte Kiddie Corral, Shingletown
Cindy Stinar Black

Brookfield Elementary School, Oakland
Linda Rogers,
Kathy Hagerty
Twila Richardson

Brookfield Head Start, Oakland
Suzie Ashley
Lola Hill
Leagun James
Betty Gibson

Cedar Creek Montessori, Berkeley
Idalina Cruz
Jeanne Devin
Len Paterson

Centro VIda, Berkeley
Rosalia Wilkins

The Child Day School, Antioch
Janice Thomas

A Child's Place, Oakley
Barbara Skaggs
Dawn-Marie Miller

Chinese Community United Methodist
Church, Oakland
Stella Ko Kwok

Christian Center School, Pittsburg
Marte Bryson

Clayton Valley Parent Preschool, Concord
Lee Ann Sanders
Patsy Sherman

Compañeros del Barrio State Preschool, San Francisco
Anastasia Decaristos
Laura Todd

Contra Costa College, San Pablo
Sylvia Alvarez-Mazzi

Country Kids Learning Center, Brentwood
Susan Galindo

Covenant Christian Preschool, Antioch
Jonni Tannenbaum

Creative Learning Center, Danville
Brooke H. B. D'Arezzo

Creative Play Center, Pleasant Hill
Sharon Keane
Debbie Coyle

Dena's Day Care, Oakland
Kawsar Elshinawy

Diane Adair Daycare Centers, Concord
Kimberly Agge
Robin Goodson

Dover Preschool, Richmond
Alice J. Romero

Duck's Nest Preschool, Berkeley
Pierrette Allison
Patricia Foster
Mara Ellen Guckian
Ruth Major

East Bay Community Children's Center, Oakland
Charlotte Johnson
Oletha R. Wade

Ecole Bilingue, Berkeley
Nichelle R. Kitt
Martha Ann Reed
Richard Mermis

Emeryville Child Development Center, Emeryville
Ortencia A. Hoopii
Ellastine Blalock
Jonetta Bradford
William L. Greene

Enrichment Plus Albert Chabot School, Oakland
Lisa Dobbs

Escondido Head Start, Escondido
Janet Quintana

Family Day Care, Oakland
Cheryl Birden
Penelope Brody
Eufemia Buena Byrd

Family Day Care, Orinda
Lucy Inouye

Family Stress Center—Head Start, Concord
Anasylvia Navarro

Gan Hillel Nursery School, Richmond
Denise Moyes-Schnur

Gan Shalom Preschool, Berkeley
Iris Greenbaum

Garner Toddler Center, Alameda
Uma Srinath

Gay Austin, Albany
Sallie Hanna-Rhyne
Zezé Cole

Giggles Family Day Care, Oakland
Doris Wührmann

Greater Richmond Social Services Corp., Richmond
Lucy Coleman

Happy Lion School, Pinole
Sharon Espinoza
Marilyn Klemm

Home Day Care, Antioch
Karen A. Ghannadan

Jack-in-the-Box Junction Preschool, Richmond
Virginia Guadarrama

Kinder–Care, Oakland
Terry Saugstad
Tara Kelly

King Child Develeopment Center, Berkeley
Margie M. Kirk

King Preschool, Richmond
Charlie M. Allums

King's Valley Christian, Concord
Pam Wofford

The Lake School, Oakland
Patricia House
Margaret Engel
Vickie Stoller

Lakeview Preschool, Oakland
Kathy Vital

Laney Childcare, Oakland
Patricia Hunter

Learning Adventures Child Development, Redding
Dena Keown

Little Promises/Christian Center, Pittsburg
Linda Tollefson

Lincoln School, Oakland
Joyce Moy

Longfellow Child Development Center, Oakland
Katryna Ray

Los Medanos Community College, Pittsburg
Judy Henry
Filomena Macedo
Doris D. Bee
Teri Limperis

Maraya's Developmental Center, Oakland
Maria A. Johnson-Price
Gayla Lucero

Mark Twain School Migrant Education, Modesto
Grace Avila

Mary Jane's Preschool, Pleasant Hill
Theresa Borges

Merritt College Children's Center, Oakland
Deborah Green
Virginia Shelton

Madroña School, Philo
Susan Munson

Mary Rocha Child Development Center, Antioch
Betty Beasley
Marilyn C. Douglas
Arleen Dumin
Matthew Heisch
Michele M. Knapp
Rosemarie Peterson
Speranza Blackard

Mickelson's Family Day Care Home, Ramona
Levata Mickelson

Mission Head Start, San Francisco
Pilar Marroquin
Mirna Torres

The Model School Comprehensive, Berkeley
Jenny Schwartz-Groody

Montclair Community Play Center, Oakland
Elaine Guttmann
Nancy Kliszewski
Mary Loeser

Moorpark College, Moorpark
Dianne K. Smith

Next Best Thing, Oakland
Denise Hingle
Franny Minervini-Zick

Oak Center Christian Academy, Oakland
Debra Booze

REVIEWERS

Oakland Parent Child Center, Oakland
Barbara Jean Jackson

Orinda Preschool, Orinda
Tracy Johansing-Spittler

Our Place, Concord
Mike Alcatraz

Oxford St. Learning Road, Berkeley
Vanna Maria Kalofonos

Peixoto Children's Center, Hayward
Alma Arias
Irma Guzman
Paula Lawrence
Tyra Toney

Pied Piper Preschool, Walnut Creek
Sherie Pedersen

Piedmont Cooperative Playschool,
Piedmont
Marcia Nybakken

Pittsburg Coordinating Preschool,
Pittsburg
Veronica Harris

Playmates Daycare, Berkeley
Mary T. McCormick

Railroad Junction School, Pittsburg
Karen E. Camp

Rainbow School, Oakland
Mary McCon
Rita Neely

St. Vincent's Day Home, Oakland
Pamela Meredith

San Antonio Head Start, Oakland
Cynthia Hammock
Ilda Terrazas

San Jose City College, San Jose
Mary Conroy

Santa Rosa Jewish Community Center
Nursery School, Santa Rosa
Jill Tager

Sequoia Nursery School, Oakland
Karen Fong

Sequoyah Community Preschool,
Oakland
Erin Smith
Kim Wilcox

Shakelford Headstart, Modesto
Teresa Avila

Sunshine Preschool, Berkeley
Poppy Richie

Ta-Share-A-Day Preschool, Oakley
Toni Teixeira

Toler Heights, Oakland
Gingee Huen

U. C. Berkeley Child Care Services Smyth
Fernwald II, Berkeley
Diane Wallace
Caroline W. Yee

Walnut Ave. Community Preschool,
Walnut Creek
Evelyn DeLanis

Washington Child Development Center,
Berkeley
Reather Jones

Washington Kids Club, Berkeley
Adwoa A. Mante

Westside Coop Preschool, San Jose
Priscilla Matusewicz

Westview Children's Center, Pacifica
Adrienne J. Schneider

Woodroe Woods, Hayward
Wendy Justice

Woodstock Child Development Center,
Alameda
Mary Raabe

Woodstock Child Development Center,
Alameda
Denise M. Ratto

Woodstock School, Alameda
Amber D. Cupples

Yuk Yan Annex, Oakland
Eileen Lok

YWCA Oakland, Oakland
Iris Ezeb
Grace Perry

YWCA, Pittsburg
Silvia Mendez

ILLINOIS
Coordinator: **Fran Donovan**

Chicago Commons-New City Child Care
Center, Chicago
Karen Haigh
Andrew Clark, Jr.
Aurora Rodriguez

Lake Shore School, Chicago
Elaine Dotson
Louisa Economou
Brenda Kay Ratts
Karen Walsh
Jean Yoshimura

LOUISIANA
Boutte Head Start, Lulins
Lisa Lauer

MASSACHUSETTS
Coordinator: **Jeri Robinson**

Joseph P. Manning Elementary School,
Jamaica Plain
Estelle Koutoulas
Elynor Harrington
Dale Hurd

Paige Academy, Roxbury
Marjorie A. Jones
Norma Yolanda Medina
Florence Agatha Moving
Chantal Latortue Pierre

MISSISSIPPI
Coordinator: **Johnnie Mills-Jones**

Edwards Elementary School, Edwards
Linda Laws
Kimberly R. Hill
Sandra Pritchard
Margaret A. Rogers
Roberta Taylor

NEW MEXICO
Coordinator: **Phyllis Etsate**

Zuni Head Start Program, Zuni
Phyllis Etsate
Bernelia Boone
Sadie Eustace
Sue Tucson

NEW YORK
Coordinator: **Marge Korzelius**

Center for the Young Child #36, Buffalo
Sandra Jean Campbell
Karen Maier
Niris L. Campbell
Jeanne B. Cooley

School 43 Annex, Buffalo
Kathleen A. Podraza
Sharon R. Chapman
Susan L. Hoyler
Jessica P. Manns

Preschool Science Collaborative, New
York
Gwendolyn Rippey

UTAH
Coordinator: **Rose Turpin**

Mountainland Head Start, Provo
Donna L. Rogers
Sheryl Schaefer
Glenna R. Schartmann
Alice Sia

CONTENTS

GEMS and PEACHES

GEMS is publishing a number of early childhood activity guides developed by the PEACHES project of the Lawrence Hall of Science. PEACHES is a curriculum development and training program for teachers and parents of children in preschool through first grade.

Like the GEMS guides already available for preschool and the early grades—such as *Hide A Butterfly*, *Animal Defenses*, and *Buzzing A Hive*—the new PEACHES guides combine free exploration, drama, art, and literature with science and mathematics to give young children positive and effective learning experiences.

INTRODUCTION

Trees are a vital part of life on Earth. Diverse varieties are all around us—in forests, orchards, and neighborhoods—creating the oxygen we breathe, providing wood, food, and paper goods, changing with the seasons, shading many of our streets. Trees are also homes to many creatures, large and small, who depend on them for shelter, warmth, and nourishment.

Tree Homes is designed to familiarize children with trees and their importance to the survival of many animals. Observations of real trees, combined with dramas and role-plays, deepen a child's appreciation for trees and the animals that live and raise families in tree homes. Life science, math, and physical science activities integrated with language arts experiences provide an appropriate and hands-on way for children to investigate the role of trees. In addition, children observe and compare the specialized features and behaviors of animals. They learn how these characteristics help animals survive in their tree hole homes.

An important life science concept emphasized in this guide is **the dependence of many animals on tree holes for warm, safe homes to raise their young.** The children become familiar with a living tree and look for live animals on it. They build a child-size tree: stacked cardboard boxes form the trunk; paper rolls with real or paper leaves become branches; and holes in the trunk become homes for toy animals.

A second important concept is that **animals have different parenting and nesting strategies**—bears use hollowed out trees as a winter den and to give birth to their cubs, raccoons use tree holes as a safe shelter for their daytime sleep, and owls use trees to build nests for their eggs and to raise their chicks. The children participate in dramas and role-plays to understand the differences and similarities of each animal's behaviors. Also, the puppets that the children create allow them to dramatize their own stories and share them later with their families in fun and meaningful ways.

Warmth is the principal physical science concept in *Tree Homes*. The children feel warmth as they role-play bear cubs snuggling together in their warm coats or raccoons curling up with their bath-towel tails wrapped around them. In the activity Getting Warmer, the children explore other ways of getting warmer. They feel heat generated by exercise, by the sun, and by friction.

Throughout the unit, the children make comparisons of animals and trees related to biology concepts. Mathematics connections also abound. Students have numerous opportunities to feel, see, touch, and compare objects using the attribute of size. For example, they compare the sizes of tree holes, the size of a mother owl to a father owl, and the size of a raccoon's tail to its body. These activities develop a vocabulary for measurement and lay the foundation for the measurement concepts they will encounter later on. In addition, the attribute of size is reinforced as children sort bears and other objects by size. Children use problem-solving and math-reasoning skills as they sort and classify objects related to trees in different ways. Number sense is developed meaningfully as children count in context while they observe animals and make puppets, as well as when they count and compare objects that are sorted.

Creative Play

Creative play activities are embedded throughout *Tree Homes*. When children play, they process new information and incorporate it into their understandings.

After presenting the dramas, leave the toy animals and drama props in the area with the cardboard tree for the children to play with during choice times. Young children, even first graders, become very involved in inventing and dramatizing their own stories, alone or with friends. The raccoon puppets and paper owls that the children make will naturally be used in their play. They may reenact realistic animal behaviors, such as nest build-

ing, searching for food, or hiding from predators, or may have the animals talk and act like humans. Often times their dramas are just plain silly. However, as they play, your students use their imaginations, develop language skills, and interact socially with one another.

Children enjoy role-playing animals and it is a wonderful way for them to learn more about them. When pretending to be bears, raccoons and owls, children must consider what animals' bodies are like, how they move, how they care for their young, and what their needs are. There are many things you can do to enhance the children's role-playing experiences. For example, put out large boxes to represent tree holes so your students can experience the shelter a real tree hole provides.

Provide plenty of time, space, and materials for creative play—and watch carefully as your students play. You will learn a lot about their interests, personalities, and developmental levels. Play is an important way for young children to understand and explore new science and mathematics content. How they play, along with stories they may draw and write with you later, will give you insight into the new ideas they have gained. When you observe children using themes from *Tree Homes* in their play, take note of the new information and concepts they are incorporating into their pretend worlds.

Activities for a Wide Range of Abilities

The activities in *Tree Homes* are for children in preschool through first grade. Because of a wide range of abilities, some of the activities are more appropriate for younger children and others for older students. It is not necessary to do every activity with each age group.

For preschoolers, select activities that the children can participate in: tasting, seeing, touching, and role playing. Keep the activities short and introduce few concepts, facts, and new words in each session. Older children can handle more discussion and more detailed observations.

Branching Off

As you and your students immerse yourselves in the topic of tree homes, the children will undoubtedly ask questions and make comments that will lead to other explorations and extension activities about trees and the animals that live in them. Be open to and listen to your students ideas and use their ideas to "branch off" from *Tree Homes*.

Children naturally relate what they learn to their real-life experiences. In one class, a child told a story about going camping and hanging a bag of food on a clothesline so the bears wouldn't get it. Because this topic was of high interest to the children, the teacher hung a clothesline in the playground and let the children practice tying up their backpacks. She also set up a tent so the children could "go camping." We encourage you to find many ways to extend the theme of tree homes into art, music, language arts, and dramatic play. Field trips and class-room visitors, both animal and human, will enrich and extend the unit.

Choices For Making Animal Puppets

An effective and enjoyable way for your students to review and understand the science and math concepts in *Tree Homes* is by making paper raccoon and owl puppets, which they can use to act out their own dramas.

The process of constructing a paper animal requires children to recall what they have learned about the animal's body structure. Children identify legs, ears, eyes, tail, and observe where they are on the body. Creating their puppet also stimulates them to think about how animals use their bodies to gather food, to protect themselves, or to build homes.

For example, while making a raccoon puppet, children may think and talk about how a real raccoon uses its tail, how sharp claws help it or why it has a mask over its eyes. You can encour-age this reflection by asking questions while the children are working. Making the paper animals is an opportune time for students to practice using new vocabulary, such as "talons," or "ear tufts." Math concepts such as counting and symmetry are also reinforced as children put legs, toes, eyes, on their animals.

Depending on your teaching approach and the skills of the children, you can choose to have the youngsters design their own raccoons and owls, or use pre-cut parts (made from the patterns in this guide). The purpose of the child- designed approach is to encourage the children's creativity. If you want to emphasize the animal's body structure, you might choose to use the pre-cut parts. Also, some teachers find the pre-cut parts helpful with students who have limited ability to use scissors.

Whichever approach you choose for making the paper ani-mals, the owls and raccoons the children create may be realistic or very imaginative. The important thing is that the children feel successful in the activity, and end up with a puppet that they can play with to enact animal behavior. Children are excited to have the raccoon and owls go in and out of the holes of the cardboard tree, or "climb" and "fly" around the classroom. The children continue to play with their paper animals at home and make up dramas to share with their families.

Activity 1

A TREE AND ITS HOLES

OVERVIEW

Children become familiar with a living tree in this activity and learn how it looks, feels, sounds, and smells. They discover that leaves make food for the tree, bark protects it, and roots bring water to the tree. The youngsters compare the texture and color of the bark to the skin on their hands. They look for holes in the tree and role-play the animals they see in the holes or on other parts of the tree.

The children help make a large cardboard tree, painting the tree and attaching real or paper leaves. They compare the sizes of the holes in the cardboard tree and also compare their tree with the living tree.

> ➤ *You could have the children make the cardboard tree in the early fall and let them add different color leaves for each of the four seasons.*

Session 1

THE LIVING TREE

WHAT YOU NEED

For the whole group

❏ Access to a living tree
❏ Several branches from living trees or bushes (or have the youngsters gather them with you on their walk). Look for branches with fruit and ones that animals have visited.

Optional
❏ Several hand lenses
❏ 1 Parts Of A Tree poster on page 23

GETTING READY

Anytime Before the Activity

1. Read the Background Information on pages 69-73 about the role of trees in nature. The information is meant to help you guide your children's thinking, but is not meant be read aloud to them.

The Living Tree

2. Find a nearby live tree in your neighborhood that you and the children can visit often.

Immediately Before the Activity

1. If you are planning to have the children tape real leaves onto the cardboard tree, look for leaves on the ground that the youngsters can gather on their walk back from the living tree. (The cardboard tree is described on page 20.)

Visiting a Living Tree

1. Take the group outdoors, and gather the children around a tree.

a. If possible, ask the children to hold hands around the tree and look from the base of the trunk up to the top of the branches. Have them move in a circle around the tree so that each child gets a different view of the tree. Ask, "What do you see on the tree?" [*branches, leaves, bark, ants*]

b. If tree roots are visible at the base of the tree ask, "Where are the roots?" Have the children observe how they come out of the tree and go into the ground.

c. Ask, "Why does a tree need roots?" Listen to the children's answers. Explain that the roots reach into the ground and bring food and water to the tree from the soil. The roots also keep the tree from falling over.

d. Have the children identify the parts of the tree (roots, trunk, branches, leaves, and bark).

2. Tell the children to close their eyes. Have them:

- feel the bark and describe how it feels.

- smell the bark and describe how it smells.

- listen to the rustle of the leaves or the creaking of the branches.

3. Have the children open their eyes and describe the colors of the bark.

4. Ask, "Why does a tree need bark?" *[for protection]* Explain that the bark helps to protect the tree, just as a heavy coat protects them from cold weather and from scratches.

5. Ask the children to compare the bark to the skin on their own hands. Ask if the bark is:

- rougher or smoother

- warmer or cooler

- wetter or drier

- darker or lighter

6. Have the children describe the colors of the leaves. Ask, "How do you think leaves help trees?" After receiving several responses, tell the group that the tree makes its own food in its leaves when the sun shines on the leaves.

7. Have the children look with you for small holes in the tree, and try to find small plants and animals, including insects, living in the holes and on other parts of the tree.

8. Suggest that the children pretend they are small animals, such as moths, butterflies, ants, or birds, like the ones they see on the tree. Encourage them to role-play flying or crawling to and from the tree.

Optional
1. Have the children help you collect branches to take back to the room.

2. If you plan to use real leaves for the cardboard tree, tell each child to choose one leaf from the ground and carry it back to the room.

3. Back in the room, display the Parts Of A Tree poster.

Observing Real Branches

1. Spread the branches out on a table, and encourage the children to look carefully at them.

2. Ask questions and give suggestions that encourage observations, such as:

   • What colors are the leaves?

   • What shapes are the leaves?

   • How do the leaves smell?

   • How do the leaves feel?

   • What animals or bugs do you see on the branch?

   • See if you can find a place where an animal has nibbled on a leaf or the branch?

Session 2

THE CARDBOARD TREE

WHAT YOU NEED

For the whole group

❏ 3 cardboard boxes with flaps to make a tree trunk (You may want to select boxes that can be nested for storage. Also, keep the tree short enough so that the children can reach the top of the tree.)
  ❏ 1 large box, at least 9" x 11" x 14"
  ❏ 1 medium box, at least 7" x 8" x 11"
  ❏ 1 small box, at least 6" x 6" x 8"
❏ 3 or more cardboard wrapping-paper rolls for tree branches (or you can use real branches)
❏ 1 container of brown poster paint
❏ 1 utility knife with a sharp, flat blade
❏ 1 8-oz. jar of white glue (or 8 large brads or about 5' of Velcro if you plan to nest the boxes for storage)
❏ 1 roll of masking tape
❏ 1 roll of double-stick tape

For each child

❏ 1 paintbrush
❏ 1 2½" x 4" rectangle (or 1 scrap) of brown, green, yellow, red, or orange paper for a leaf (or you can use a real leaf)

   #### Optional
   ❏ 1 pair of scissors

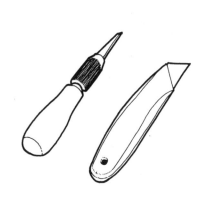

➤ *We found that the Making a Cardboard Tree activity works best in groups of 12 children or less. That way every child gets a chance to help construct the tree.*

GETTING READY

Anytime Before the Activity

1. Prepare the paper for paper leaves (or you can use real leaves). Cut the paper into 2½" x 4" rectangles, one for each child (the children will use these to make leaves during the activity), or use scraps of colored paper for the children to tear into leaf shapes.

Several Days Before the Activity

1. Use the cardboard boxes to make a tree trunk and the wrapping-paper rolls to make branches, or use real branches. Use the sharp knife to cut one hole in each box.

Note: The holes need to be distinctly different in size. The owl is designed to fit into the small hole, the raccoon in the middle-size hole, and a bear family into the large hole. Therefore, carefully follow the instructions below.

a. Cut one oval-shaped hole in the large box. Make it at least 8" wide and 12" high.

b. Use pattern A on page 49 to cut one hole in the medium box.

c. Use pattern B on page 62 to cut one hole in the small box.

d. Save the cardboard ovals you cut from the holes. You will use them in Tree Hole Sizes on page 21.

e. Cut one small hole for each branch in the small box. Cut the holes on the sides of the box that don't have flaps.

f. Use the masking tape to tape down the flaps of the boxes.

Optional
Cut roots from the flaps of the large box.

The Cardboard Tree

Making the Cardboard Tree

1. Ask the children to recall their visit to the live tree. What did the tree look like? Review the parts of the tree including the trunk, branches, leaves, and roots. What animals did they find on the tree? What else was special about the tree?

2. Show the boxes and the paper rolls to the children, and tell them they are going to make a cardboard tree to keep in the room. Have the youngsters stack the boxes from the biggest on the bottom to the smallest on the top to see what the tree trunk will look like. Ask, "What part of the tree can the paper rolls be?" [branches]

3. Have the children paint the boxes and the paper rolls brown. Leave them for several hours or overnight for the paint to dry.

4. When the paint is dry, glue the boxes together, or fasten with velcro or brads. The children can help you put the boxes together.

5. If you use glue, leave the boxes undisturbed for several hours or overnight until the glue is dry.

6. Let the children insert the branches into the small, pre-cut holes.

Attaching Leaves

1. If you plan to use paper leaves for the tree, show the children how to tear the paper or cut the corners off the paper to make leaves. Have the youngsters make their leaves.

2. Show the youngsters how to tape the real or paper leaves to the tree. Then have the children attach them to the tree.

Comparing the Real and Cardboard Tree

1. Encourage the children to talk about the real tree. Have them review what they saw, felt, heard, and smelled when they were standing around the real tree.

2. Show the children the cardboard tree and have them identify its parts (trunk, branches, and leaves). Ask, "How is our tree different from the real tree we visited?" Encourage comparisons, such as:

   - taller or shorter
   - round trunk or square trunk
   - rougher or smoother
   - holes or no holes
   - small holes or big holes

3. Ask, "Have you ever seen a real tree with big holes?" "How do you think the big holes are made?" After taking several responses, explain that a branch can fall off a tree leaving a hole that gets bigger, or an animal can make a hole in a tree.

Tree Hole Sizes
(for preschool and kindergarten)

1. Gather the children on the floor in a half circle in front of the cardboard tree.

2. Encourage them to compare the holes in the cardboard tree, taking turns finding a big, middle-size, and small hole.

3. When they find the middle-size hole, ask a child to find a bigger hole, then a smaller one.

4. Ask, "Where is the smallest hole?" "The biggest hole?" "The middle-size hole?" Ask for a volunteer to point to each hole.

➤ *One teacher attached a paper leaf at each end of a short string so that the children could drape the leaves over a branch and rearrange them.*

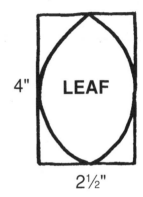

4" LEAF

2½"

➤ *One class covered the cardboard tree trunk with paper mache before painting it to give it the look and texture of real bark.*

The Cardboard Tree

5. Show the children the three oval-shaped pieces that you cut from the boxes. Have the children match each piece to its corresponding hole size in the cardboard tree.

GOING FURTHER

1. Frequently visit the same living tree to find out if the tree has changed.
   • Are there fewer or more leaves, sprouts, or branches?
   • Is there more evidence of animal visits (nibbled leaves, bark, new ant trails, stored food)?
   • Are roots visible?
   • Has the tree's color or texture changed?
   • How many animal homes can you find on the tree?
   Have the children think about and share why these changes happened.

2. Bring the cardboard tree into the room during each of the four seasons so the children can add different color leaves for the fall, winter, spring, and summer. They can add buds and flowers in the spring, and fruit during the summer and early fall.

3. Let the children help you plant a living tree and watch it grow.

4. Bring in young shoots from trees, place them in water, and let the children watch the buds develop.

5. Take the children to a nursery with tree seedlings, an arboretum, or a forest preserve.

➤ *One teacher had the children look around the room for products that come from trees, such as the door or table. The youngsters may know that the cardboard for the classroom tree came from a real tree.*

➤ *Another teacher set up a "store" in the classroom. She had the children bring from home items that come from trees—such as a bunch of bananas, a bottle of orange juice, a can of apple sauce, paper, and wood products—to put in the store.*

➤ *A third teacher had the children write or dictate letters to their grandparents asking them to send leaves from trees that are near their homes. The grandparents sent pictures and information about the trees. The teacher laminated the leaves and had the children sort, graph, and display them.*

PARTS OF A TREE

Activity 2

BLACK BEARS

OVERVIEW

Black Bears begins with a short drama about a mother bear and her playful cubs. The children learn that baby bears are born during the cold winter months; bears eat grasshoppers, nuts, and berries; and bears climb trees for safety. The girls and boys role-play bear-cub behavior, including snuggling together to stay warm. The children bring toy bears from home, which they first use for dramas and then for a sorting and classifying activity. They continue to sort and classify, using things that are related to trees such as nuts, leaves, wooden objects, and fruits.

Session 1

BEAR DRAMA AND ROLE PLAYING

WHAT YOU NEED

For the whole group

- ❏ 1 large cardboard tree
- ❏ 2 or more large toy bears
  (The bears should fit through the largest tree hole.)
- ❏ 1 or more small toy bears
- ❏ 1 large brown paper bag
- ❏ Several acorns, nuts, and/or berries
- ❏ 1 toy grasshopper or other insect
- ❏ Large boxes, blankets, or bedspreads

GETTING READY

Anytime Before the Activity

Read Bears in the Background Information section on page 70.

Several Days Before the Activity

1. For this activity you need at least three toy bears, preferably two large ones and a small one. Ask the children to bring toy bears from home, if they have any, for the science lesson.

2. Send notes to parents letting them know that the children are learning about bears. Tell the parents that you have asked the children who have toy bears to bring them to class for the science lesson. Ask the parents to label the bear with the child's name.

Immediately Before the Activity

1. Place the cardboard tree on the floor.

2. Create caves by draping blankets or bedspreads over tables, or by setting up large boxes.

Playing With Bears

1. When the boys and girls bring their toy bears from home, allow time to play freely with the bears.

2. Let the children play with the bears in the tree holes.

The Bear Drama

1. Set up the room for The Bear Drama.

- Place the cardboard tree in a section of the room where everyone can see the drama.

- Put one or two small toy bears in the largest tree hole. Hide them behind the folded brown paper bag so that the children can't see them. The two large toy bears can be the mother and father bears. Place them near the tree.

- Place acorns, nuts, and/or berries on the floor in front of the tree, and hide the toy grasshopper somewhere near the tree.

Optional
- If the children bring more than four toy bears to class, use these bears for the Optional Cave Drama (see page 27). Hide the additional bears in the "caves" in groups of three or four. Include a large mother bear in each group.

2. Gather the children around the cardboard tree, and present a drama of a father bear, mother bear, and their cubs. Tell a story as you act out the drama.

- Two big bears sniff around the ground under the tree, looking for good things to eat. They gulp down some acorns (nuts and/or berries). They are eating as much food as they can, preparing for their long winter rest.

> ➤ *The children become much more involved in the dramas and role playing when they play with the bears they bring from home.*

- The days get colder. The big father bear wanders off into the woods to look for a warm, safe place to sleep.

- The mother bear finds a large hole in a big tree, and goes inside to sleep for several months.

- During the cold winter, baby bears are born. They all keep warm by snuggling close together in the hole.

- In the spring when the weather gets warm, the mother bear comes out of her tree hole. Look what's following her. (Count the baby bears with the children as you "walk" the cubs out of the hole.)

- What is a name for a baby bear? [cub]

- The mother bear takes her cubs to look for good things to eat. They find grasshoppers in the grass. (Hop the toy grasshopper in front of a bear cub and pretend the cub is eating it.)

- She shows her cubs how to climb a tree. One of the cubs is afraid to come down, and the mother helps it.

- The cubs like to play. They roll over on the ground together and stand on their hind legs.

- The mother sniffs the air. She hears a sound, a rustle in the bushes. She cries "woof," and all the bears scurry up the tree. When it is safe, they slowly, cautiously climb down again.

- As night approaches, the air becomes cold. The bears go into their tree hole and snuggle together to stay warm.

Optional Cave Drama
- Use the additional bears brought from home. Have the bears in the cave come out "during the spring," look for food, play, go back into the cave, and snuggle together to stay warm.

Role-Playing Bears

1. Divide the class into groups of three or four children. Encourage the children to pretend to be bear cubs and snuggle together in the "caves" to stay warm.

2. Allow time for the children to continue role-playing bears and to play with the toy bears.

GOING FURTHER

Bring in books with good illustrations or photographs of other types of bears, such as grizzly bears and polar bears. (See Resource Books on page 75. Compare those bears with the Bear poster of a black bear on page 33.)

➤ *If children have not had a chance to play with each other's bears to some extent before this activity, you may want to allow some free play time with the bears so that the children can focus on the sorting activity.*

Session 2

SORTING BEARS

WHAT YOU NEED

For each child and yourself

❑ 1 toy bear (Be sure to have extra bears available for those children who do not bring one.)

Sorting Bears

1. Have the children bring their bears to the group area in the room. Sit in a circle and have each child introduce her bear to the other children. This will give the children an opportunity to look at each of the bears before the sorting activity begins.

2. Ask the children for their observations about the bears. Accept all responses. If necessary, guide the children into making observations about the attributes of the bears, such as color, size, type of bear, texture, realistic, imaginary, etc., by asking leading questions.

3. As *color* is a clear, easy way to sort, start by sorting the bears by color. Ask, "What colors are the bears?" As a child suggests a color, have a bear that color placed inside the circle of children. Then ask for another color. Again, place one bear of that color inside the circle of children. Continue until all the colors of the bears are named.

4. Going around the circle of children, have each child, one by one, put her bear inside the circle next to the bear(s) whose color matches hers. When everyone has placed his bear, look at the groups of bears. Review the colors of bears.

5. Ask questions about the groups of bears, such as "How many

> *One teacher helped his preschoolers understand color sorting by saying, "If your bear is brown, stand up." (All the children with brown bears stood together.) "If your bear is white, stand up." He continued until all the colors were sorted.*

> *Some children may have multicolored bears. This will give children an opportunity to do some problem solving. Ask children where to place multicolored bears. If a bear is predominantly one color, they may suggest placing it in an established color group. Other times, children have created a multicolored category and all the multicolored bears are placed there. It is important that the children choose the appropriate group for their bears.*

Sorting Bears

bears are brown?" Then count the brown bears. Next, ask comparative questions, such as: "What color group has the most bears?" or "What color group has smallest number of bears?" or "Are there any groups with the same number of bears?"

➤ *Some teachers use the tree holes to sort the bears by size. Each child compares her bear to the tree holes and places it inside the tree hole that the bear best matches in size. In cases of really large bears, the children can place the bear outside of the tree.*

6. After the children have made all the observations possible, have them, one by one, take back their bears.

7. Depending upon their abilities and interests, sort the bears in a new way. The children have already been working with comparative size in the tree activity, so you may want to sort by size. Tell the children that they are going to put their bears in groups by their size.

8. Ask the children what sizes their bears are. As they suggest a size, such as "big," ask for a bear that is big and put it inside the circle of children. Ask what other size bears there are. Again, ask for a bear that is that size and put it in the circle away from the big bear. Continue to ask for words to describe the size of the bears until all the sizes have been named.

9. After the sizes are established, go around the circle of children and have each child, one by one, put his bear inside the circle next to the bear(s) whose size it matches.

➤ *One teacher said her first graders enjoyed arranging their bears into bar graphs.*

10. Review the size groups of bears. Ask for observations about the groups. Count the number of bears in each group. Ask additional questions about the bears in the group, such as "What group has the most bears?" or "What group has the smallest number of bears?" or "Do any groups have the same number of bears?"

11. As time and interest permits, ask the children for additional ways to sort the bears. They may suggest sorting by realistic and imaginary bears, bears with hats and bears without hats, or tails and no tails. Select one of their attributes and sort again!

➤ *It is important to use the children's size words to create the categories for the bears. For example, some children may only see two groups—big and little—to classify the bears, while other children may suggest four categories, such as large, medium, small, and tiny.*

GOING FURTHER: MORE SORTS

Nut Sort

1. Collect a variety of nuts that are still in their shells. Children can bring in nuts from home. Be sure to have several of each type of nut—at least four varieties such as walnuts, almonds, pecans, peanuts, Brazil nuts, hazel nuts (filberts), and acorns.

2. Gather the children in a circle. Hold up a nut they might be familiar with such as a walnut. Ask if anyone knows what kind of nut it is. Once the walnut is identified, ask where it came from. *[a tree]*

3. Pass walnuts around for the children to handle. Have them describe its attributes. *[brown, bumpy, round, pointed]*

4. Hold up another nut and ask if anyone recognizes it. Again, identify it and have children describe its attributes. Continue in a similar manner with the other nuts.

5. After all nuts have been named, place them in one group in the center of the circle of children. Ask the children how the nuts can be sorted. They may suggest sorting by type, size, shape, texture, or another attribute. Do at least one sort they suggest. For example, if the children suggest sorting by type of nut, sort into types.

6. After sorting, ask number and comparison questions about the number of nuts in each group, such as:

    How many almonds are there?

    Are there more walnuts or peanuts? How many more?

7. As time and interest permit, sort the nuts a second time using another attribute and compare the groups.

8. Students may want to crack open the nuts and examine the meat inside. If students are going to sample the nuts, be sure to check if any students are allergic to nuts as some allergies can be very severe.

Leaf Sort

Have children collect leaves from the school environment as well as from their home environments. Generate a list of attributes to describe the leaves and sort them several ways.

Wood Sort

Have each child bring in an object from home that is made from wood. After each child shares the object with the class at circle time, place objects in the center of the circle. Ask children for their ideas on how to sort the objects. Sort the wooden objects in at least one way. Reinforce the idea that all the wooden objects are made from trees.

Fruit Sort

Fruits from trees are another interesting item to sort. Apple season is a particularly good time to have each child bring in an apple. It is likely you will get red, green, and yellow varieties of apples. Children can sort and graph the apples by color. They can also use shape or type of apple to sort.

Another fruit sort can be done by asking the children to bring in one piece of fruit. You can sort the fruit in many ways including whether it grew on trees or not. The fruit can then be used to make a fruit salad. This gives children a chance to see the different types of seeds in each fruit.

Treasure Boxes

For more sorting activities and challenges, you may wish to check out the GEMS guide *Treasure Boxes* for grades K–3.

BEAR

Activity 3

GETTING WARMER

OVERVIEW

The children explore the many ways people and animals keep warm. They review how bears snuggle together in a tree to stay warm, and learn how thick coats keep animals—and people— warm. They experience the heat generated by the sun, by friction, and by jumping up and down.

WHAT YOU NEED

For the whole group

- ❏ Child-size warm clothing:
  - ❏ 1 sweater
  - ❏ 1 coat
  - ❏ 1 sock
  - ❏ 1 glove
  - ❏ 1 hat
  - ❏ 1 scarf
- ❏ 1 or more blankets
- ❏ 1 large box or paper bag

  #### Optional
  - ❏ 1 large sheet of paper at least 12" x 18"
  - ❏ Watercolor markers or crayons in a variety of colors

For each child

- ❏ 1 coat

GETTING READY

Several Days Before the Activity

For this activity, each child needs a warm coat. Send a note home asking parents to send coats with their children on the day of the activity.

> ➤ *A kindergarten teacher from Alaska found these Getting Warmer activities a good time to talk about keeping warm in an emergency, such as when the power goes out or when you are stuck in a stalled car on the road.*

Immediately Before the Activity

1. Hide the warm child-size clothing in a large cardboard box, and place the box in the area where you present the activity.

2. The children may suggest items that you don't have. In case they do, consider drawing quick sketches of these items. Have some paper and a marker near the box.

> ➤ *Hiding the clothes in a box stimulates the children to think about clothing that keeps them warm because they are curious about what is in the box.*

What Clothes Keep You Warm?

1. Gather the children in a circle on the floor. Review how bear cubs get warm. *[snuggling together, having fur, hiding in a hole in a tree]*

2. Ask, "How do you keep warm?" If a child suggests a coat, pull a coat out of the box and put it in the middle of the circle.

3. If the children have trouble thinking of things, give a few hints. Say, "What can you wear on your head (or neck or feet) to keep you warm?"

4. Allow plenty of time for the children to come up with ideas. Continue to put the objects in the circle as the children suggest them. Continue to give hints.

5. If the children suggest objects that you do not have in the box, you could quickly draw those objects on the paper. Keep the paper in the middle of the circle so that everyone can see all of the objects.

6. Count all the objects with the children and put them back in the box.

Snuggling

1. Ask, "What can you snuggle under to get warm?" If a child suggests blankets, let the children snuggle up under blankets.

2. Have the children put on their coats. Ask, "Are you getting warmer?"

3. Tell them that now they are like little bears with warm coats. Ask, "What else could the little bears do to get even warmer with their coats on?" *[get in a cave, snuggle together]* Make caves by draping blankets over tables. Let the children snuggle in the caves. Ask, "Are you getting warmer?"

➤ *One teacher noticed that her children were more willing to wear their jackets outside in cold weather after doing the Getting Warmer activities.*

Being Active

1. Gather the children in a circle. Ask, "Are you warmer when you stand still or when you jump up and down?"

2. Encourage them to jump up and down to find out.

3. Ask, "How else can you move to get warmer?" [*hop, run*] As the children make suggestions, have them try out their ideas.

Sun Activity

Do the following activity in a room where the sun shines directly on the floor or on a table, or do it outside on a hot day.

1. Have the children find a sunny place and hold their hands out in the sun. Ask, "How do your hands feel?" [*warm*]

2. Have the children find an area that is not in the sun and gather there. Ask, "Do your hands feel warmer when they are in the sun or out of the sun?" [*in the sun*]

3. Tell the children that animals, plants, and other things get warmer when they are in the sun.

Friction

1. Briskly rub your hands together. Have the children rub their hands together.

2. Ask, "What happens?" [*hands get warmer*] If the children's answers are not focused on getting warmer, ask, "Does rubbing make your hands get warmer?"

3. Ask, "What else can you rub to get warmer?" [*arms, legs*] Have the children try out their suggestions.

GOING FURTHER

1. Ask, "What are other things you can do to get warmer?" If a boy says that cocoa makes him warm, let the children sip warm cocoa, warm water, or soup. If a girl says that holding warm things makes her warm, let the children hold a cup of cold water and then a cup of warm water, and compare them. You can also let them hold balloons or hot water bottles filled with warm water.

➤ *A teacher added real objects that keep you warm to the playhouse area. She included clothing for snow, wind, and rain.*

2. Ask the children to bring from home toy animals or pictures of animals with fur. Encourage the youngsters to feel the fur on live classroom animals, such as rats and guinea pigs.

3. Work with a small group of children, and encourage the children to think of ways that they get warm. After they practice acting out their ideas, encourage them to perform for others. The other children can guess what they are doing. Some ideas the children may suggest are:

   • drinking cocoa

   • warming hands in front of a fire, heater, or dryer

   • putting on warm clothes to go out to play

   • hugging each other

   • running in place

4. Do activities in which heat is involved, such as melting chocolate, melting wax, heating soup, and baking cookies.

5. Suggest the children dress a doll in warm clothes.

➤ *One teacher started a "Getting Warmer" bulletin board. She asked the children to find in the classroom, or bring from home, pictures or clothing that showed getting warmer. She also encouraged them to draw pictures of warm clothing. The children who could use scissors cut out pictures for the bulletin board.*

➤ *Another teacher started a "Getting Warmer" flannel board. She cut a figure of a child and warm clothes out of felt (coat, hat, mittens, scarf, and boots) and the children dressed the cut-out figure in the warm clothes.*

Activity 4

RACCOONS

OVERVIEW

The Raccoons activity begins with a drama about a raccoon that makes its home in a tree hole. While watching the drama, the children learn that raccoons climb trees, sleep during the day, hunt for food at night, and eat a variety of food, including worms, berries, corn, fish, and nuts. The children also learn that a tree hole provides a warm, safe, and well-hidden place for a home.

The children continue working with measurement as they find a tree hole that is the right size for the raccoon to enter. They compare the size of the raccoon's small tail with its big body as they look at The Raccoon poster.

While looking at the poster, the children count the raccoon's legs, toes, and stripes on its tail. They make paper-bag raccoons and give them four legs and tail stripes. The children play with their paper raccoons and role-play real raccoon behavior.

Session 1

GETTING TO KNOW RACCOONS

WHAT YOU NEED

For the whole group

- ❏ 1 large cardboard tree
- ❏ 1 toy raccoon that fits into the middle-sized hole of the cardboard tree, or a raccoon puppet
- ❏ 1 toy garbage can, or a plastic container, preferably with a lid
- ❏ 1 poster of The Raccoon
- ❏ Several warm adult sweaters, small quilts, bath towels, or child-size blankets
- ❏ Old socks
- ❏ Face paint or black crepe paper

> ➤ *To make a raccoon puppet for the drama, see page 47.*

Optional
- ❏ Raccoon pictures (See Resource Books on page 75.)
- ❏ Flashlight or small lamp

GETTING READY

Anytime Before the Activity

Read Raccoons in the Background Information section on page 71.

Immediately Before the Activity

Put the cardboard tree in the section of the room where you gather the children for The Raccoon Drama. Place the toy or puppet raccoon near the tree and the garbage can nearby (perhaps near the area where the children play house).

Introducing The Raccoon

1. Gather the children on the floor in a half circle in front of the cardboard tree.

2. Say, "I am thinking of an animal that has fur, a black mask, and stripes on its tail. What is it?" *[a raccoon]*

3. Show the girls and boys the toy or puppet raccoon.

4. Allow time for the children to take turns telling the class about their experiences with raccoons.

The Raccoon Drama

Partially darken the room. Tell a story and act out a short drama about a raccoon that comes to the tree looking for a hole in which to make its home. You may want to shine a flashlight or use a lamp to represent moonlight as you tell the story.

- Late one night a raccoon wanders over to the tree. It looks at the large tree hole. It is a big hole. Is the hole bigger or smaller than the raccoon? *[bigger]*

- The raccoon sniffs the hole. (Have the children sniff.) It smells the bear.

- It quickly climbs to the top of the tree and finds a small hole. Is this hole bigger or smaller than the raccoon? *[smaller]* The hole is so small that the raccoon can't crawl into it.

- The raccoon climbs down the tree still looking for a hole that is just the right size. Where do you see a hole that is big enough for the raccoon to go inside? (Let a child place the raccoon in the middle-size hole.)

- The sun comes up. It is early morning and the raccoon goes inside the hole to sleep for the rest of the day.

- That night the raccoon comes out of its hole, climbs down the tree, and goes off looking for food. It digs for worms under the tree, nibbles berries as it walks through the forest, and wanders over to a house that is near the forest.

- Outside of a house the raccoon finds a garbage can. It climbs on the can and, with its long fingers, the raccoon carefully lifts the lid and slides inside. It eats corn and fish left over from someone's dinner.

- Just then the raccoon hears the loud barking of a dog from inside the house. The raccoon quickly climbs out of the garbage can and hurries back to the forest. Where can the raccoon hide? *[In the tree hole]* Inside the hole, the raccoon is safe and well-hidden.

- Once again the raccoon climbs out of its hole and down the tree. This time it finds some nuts to eat under a nut tree.

- The raccoon begins to get very cold and tired. Just before the sun comes up, it quietly returns to its home, crawls in, curls up with its tail wrapped around it to keep warm, and goes to sleep.

The Raccoon Poster

1. Show The Raccoon poster to the group and have the children find the raccoon's mask, eyes, ears, nose, whiskers, tail, and fur.

2. Ask, "Why do you think a raccoon has a mask?" Accept the children's ideas. Explain that a black mask makes it harder for other animals to see the raccoon's eyes.

3. Have the youngsters count the raccoon's legs and toes.

4. Ask, "How many toes do you have on your foot?" "How is your foot like the raccoon's?" *[same number of toes]*

5. Have the youngsters count the black stripes on the raccoon's tail. Ask, "Is the raccoon's tail bigger or smaller than the raccoon's body?" *[smaller]*

6. Ask, "What does a raccoon have to keep it warm? *[fur, long furry tail]*
"What else can a raccoon do to keep warm?" *[stay in a hole or cave, wrap its tail around itself, stay in a warm, sunny place]*

Raccoon Creative Play

1. To extend the Getting Warmer activities, encourage the children to be raccoons and curl up in a warm place (under a blanket-covered table or in a cardboard box) with "raccoon tails" wrapped around them. The tails can be adult sweaters, small quilts, bath towels, or child-size blankets tied around the children's waists or tucked into their pants. The children will feel the warmth and understand how a furry tail can keep an animal warm.

2. The children can make raccoon masks and tails to wear. They can make the masks out of black paper, or use face paint. The tails can be made from old socks or paper, and painted with black stripes. The children can crawl into "tree holes" (large cardboard boxes or under tables). If trees with low branches are available and safe, let the "raccoons" climb the trees.

GOING FURTHER

1. Display pictures of squirrels, foxes, cats, or other animals with furry tails, or use toy animals to demonstrate how these animals use their tails to stay warm.

Session 2

RACCOON SNACKS

WHAT YOU NEED

For each child

❏ 1 paper lunch bag
❏ Several berries, apple slices, nuts, and possibly a few cooked noodles

Raccoon Snacks

1. At snack time, partially darken the room and pretend with your group that it is late at night and all of you are raccoons looking for food.

2. Give each child a paper lunch bag containing raccoon food, such as several berries, apple slices, nuts, and possibly a few cooked noodles as worms. Without looking inside the bags, encourage the children to feel inside and guess what each item is.

3. Let the group of hungry "raccoons" eat their snacks.

Session 3

MAKING PAPER-BAG RACCOONS

CHOICES FOR MAKING RACCOONS

The children make raccoon puppets and act out real raccoon behavior as they play with the puppets.

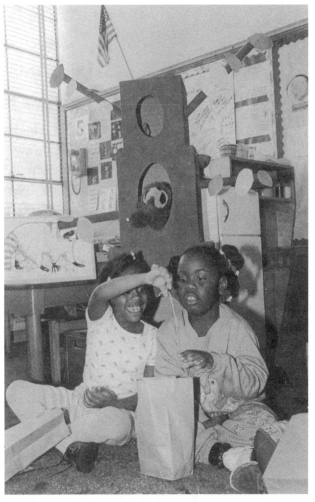

By creating a paper-bag raccoon, children review important science concepts as well as making a puppet to use in their own dramas. The process of constructing a paper animal requires children to recall what they have learned about the raccoon's body structure. Children identify legs, ears, eyes, tail, and observe where they are on the body. Creating their puppet also stimulates them to think about how the raccoon uses their body to gather food, to keep themselves warm, or to hide from predators.

Depending on your teaching approach and the skills of the children, you can choose to have the youngsters design their own raccoons or use pre-cut parts. The purpose of the child-designed approach is to encourage the children's creativity. If you want to emphasize the animal's body structure, you might choose to use the pre-cut parts. Also, some teachers find the pre-cut parts helpful with students who have limited ability to use scissors.

Whichever approach you choose for making the puppet, the raccoon the children create may be realistic or very imaginative. The important thing is that the children feel successful in the activity, and end up with a puppet that they can play with to enact animal behavior.

WHAT YOU NEED

For the whole group

❏ 1 tray
❏ Newspapers, enough to cover the tray and work tables
❏ 1 large pair of scissors

Optional
❏ 1 role of transparent tape

For each child and yourself

❏ 1 sheet of 5" x 6" brown construction paper
❏ 1 black crayon (or marker)
❏ Paste or glue
❏ 1 paper lunch bag
❏ 1 handful of brown yarn cut into 1" to 3" pieces

➤ *Some teachers had the children draw ears on their raccoons.*

GETTING READY

Anytime Before the Activity

1. Cut construction paper for the raccoon's tail, legs, and ears (see drawings on this page). You need one sheet of 5" x 6" brown construction paper for each child and for yourself. Cut the paper for each raccoon into the following sizes:

    • 1 piece 3" x 6" (1 tail)

    • 4 pieces 1" x 3" (4 legs)

    • 2 pieces 1" x 1" (2 ears)

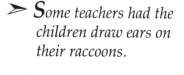

2. Use the patterns on page 49 to cut out the raccoon's tail (Pattern D) and ears (Pattern C). The ears can be cut from paper scraps. Then fold the ears at the bottom. (See the drawings on this page.)

Optional
1. Round off the open end of the bags to make them look like raccoon rear ends. (See the drawing on this page.)

2. Tape down the four corners on the bottom of the bags to give each raccoon a pointed face.

Immediately Before the Activity

1. Spread newspapers on the tables and place paste, one black crayon, one paper bag, four legs, two ears, and one tail at each child's place.

2. Place a tray with newspaper, paste, black crayon, and paper raccoon body parts in the area where you present the activity.

Making Raccoon Puppets

1. Have the children help you make a paper raccoon.

   • Write your name on one side of the paper bag and turn it over to add the other parts.
   • Have a child find the raccoon's head and mouth.
   • Ask, "What does a raccoon have on its face?" *[Eyes, Mask]* Draw the raccoon's eyes and a mask around the eyes. Also, draw other features that the boys and girls mention, such as a nose or whiskers.
   • Draw or glue on the raccoon's ears.
   • Count the legs with the group as you glue the legs onto the body.
   • Have a child show you where to put the tail. Glue the tail onto the body.
   • Count the stripes with the children as you draw seven black stripes on the raccoon's tail.
   • Ask, "What does the raccoon have on its body to keep it warm?" *[Fur]* Pretend the yarn is fur and glue it onto the raccoon's body.

2. Send the children to the tables to make their raccoons.

3. Write the children's names on their raccoons if the children are unable to write their own names.

Creative Play

Allow plenty of free time for the children to play with their paper raccoons. This time allows the children to review and understand the importance of tree homes for raccoons through drama and storytelling. Encourage children to dictate and illustrate stories about their raccoons. You may want to put various toy foods that raccoons like to eat around the cardboard tree, put out a clean garbage can, and have a toy dog available for the children to use in their play. Send the puppets home with a note encouraging creative play with family members.

➤ *One kindergarten teacher noticed the puppets tearing so the children stuffed them with newspaper and sealed them.*

RACCOON

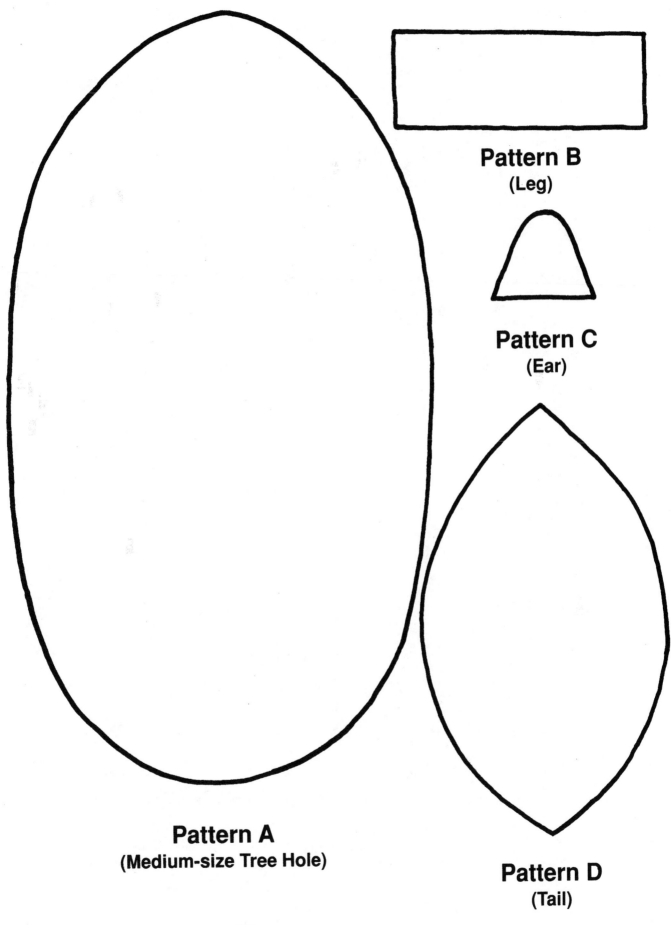

Pattern B
(Leg)

Pattern C
(Ear)

Pattern A
(Medium-size Tree Hole)

Pattern D
(Tail)

PATTERNS

Activity 5

OWLS

OVERVIEW

Children are introduced in this activity to another animal that makes its home in a tree—an owl. Through dramatic play, children see how mother and father owls build a nest together in a small tree hole. The owls lay eggs in nests made of sticks, hunt at night, and eat mice and snakes.

In other sessions, children explore the special characteristics of owls, and how these features help them survive in a forest. Children discover why owls have big eyes, large wings, sharp claws, and heads that can face backwards. They compare the sizes of the parent owls, and learn that mother owls are larger than father owls. They also find a tree hole that is the same size and the paper mother owl.

The children make owls that live in paper-bag tree homes. As their owl peeks out from holes, the children perform a finger play about an owl and its nighttime behaviors. The concept of trees providing shelter, warmth, and a safe place to raise young are emphasized throughout.

Session 1

GETTING TO KNOW OWLS

WHAT YOU NEED

For the whole group

- ❏ 1 large cardboard tree
- ❏ 2 toy owls (one slightly larger than the other) that fit into the top hole of the cardboard tree, or make two paper owls.
- ❏ 1 toy mouse, or paper mouse (Pattern K on page 63)
- ❏ 1 toy snake, or paper snake (Pattern L on page 63)
- ❏ 1 poster of The Owl
- ❏ Several feathers
- ❏ 1 lunch bag full of small sticks
- ❏ 1 handful of real or paper leaves
- ❏ Owl pictures (See Resource Books on page 75.)

  #### Optional
  - ❏ Flashlight or small lamp

➤ *To make a paper owl, see page 54.*

GETTING READY

Anytime Before the Activity

Read Owls in the Background Information section on page 72.

Optional

1. If you do not have two toy owls to use in the drama, see the instructions on page 54 to make two paper owls. Make the father owl smaller than the mother by trimming an owl body and two wings. (See the drawings on this page.)

2. If you do not have a toy mouse and snake to use in the drama, use the patterns on page 63 to cut out a paper mouse (Pattern K) and paper snake (Pattern L).

Immediately Before the Activity

1. Place the cardboard tree in the section of the room where you gather the children for discussions and dramas. Have the paper parent owls near the tree.

2. To prepare for The Owl Drama, scatter small sticks and leaves on the ground in front of the tree. Hide the paper mouse and snake under the leaves.

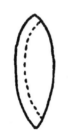

The Owl Poster

1. Ask, "I'm thinking of another animal that lives in hole in a tree—and this one flies around quietly at night! What do you think it is?" *[bird, bat, insects]* Allow time for children to share their stories about the animals they suggest.

2. Show the owl poster and say, "This is a special kind of bird." (Pause before naming the owl to let children who might recognize it call out its name.) "An owl." Allow children to share what they know about owls. Ask more questions to encourage children to think about the many specialized functions of an owl's big eyes, sharp claws, pointed beak, and long feathers.

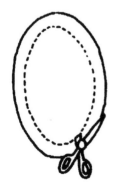

3. Ask a child to find the owl's eyes. Ask, "How do you think big eyes help owls?" *[big eyes help owls to see better when hunting at night]*

4. Explain that owls can turn their heads all the way around to see what's behind them. Encourage the children to turn their heads to see if they can see what's behind them.

5. Have the children find the nostrils on the owl's beak, its wings, and its sharp claws. Have the children count the claws.

Real Feathers

1. Ask, "What does the owl have all over its wings and body that is very soft?" *[feathers]*

2. Pass the feathers around for the children to touch.

3. Ask, "How do you think feathers help owls?" If the children don't know, tell them that feathers help keep the owl warm.

4. Explain that the tufts on top of the owl's head are feathers, not ears. Show the class where the owl's ears are (hidden under feathers on the sides of the owl's head).

Comparisons

1. Gather the children on the floor in a half circle in front of the cardboard tree.

2. "Fly" the mother and father owls in front of the group. Hold them upright on the floor with wings folded and ask, "Which owl is bigger?" Have a child point to the larger owl. Tell the class that mother owls are bigger than father owls. Ask, "Which owl do you think is the mother owl?" Have a child point to the mother owl.

3. Ask a child to find a tree hole that is the same size as the mother owl. *[the smallest hole]* Have the child fit the owl into the hole.

The Owl Drama

With the children in a half circle in front of the cardboard tree, present a short nighttime drama of parent owls making their home in the smallest tree hole. Darken the room and pretend it is nighttime. You may wish to use a flashlight or small lamp to represent the moon as you tell the story. Tell the story as you act out the drama.

- It is a dark cold night with a full moon.

- The father owl flies to the tree hole. He closes his wings and moves into the hole.

- The mother and father owls peep out of the hole.

- They fly to the ground and pick up sticks with their beaks or claws. They fly with the sticks to the hole. What do you think they are doing with the sticks? [building a nest in the hole]

- The mother owl lays an egg. Mother owls lay eggs several days apart. Several days go by and the owl lays another egg. She sits on the nest, keeping the eggs warm.

- The father owl's big eyes search the ground for food. Suddenly, he swoops down from the hole, picks up a mouse with his claws, and carries it to the mother owl to eat.

- Several days go by. The father owl sees a small snake in the leaves under the tree. He catches the snake and takes it back to the nest. The hungry mother owl gobbles up the snake.

- Both parents sit in the nest. They hold their wings close to their bodies and snuggle together to stay warm.

Creative Play

Encourage the children to play with the cardboard tree and the animals from the drama.

Owl Pictures

1. Have books with large owl pictures in the room for the children to see the variety of owls.

2. Have them compare the owls and identify the owl parts.

Session 2

MAKING PAPER OWLS

CHOICES FOR MAKING PAPER OWLS

The children make paper owls to "fly" in and out of their paper-bag trees, and for other creative-play activities. Depending on your teaching approach and the skills of the children, you may choose to have the youngsters make very simple owls, design their own owls, or follow the directions for making owls that focus on owl body structure.

The Simple Owl

Three-year-old children can make very simple paper owls by putting on eyes, gluing on wings and a beak, and drawing other owl parts if they choose. (See the accompanying drawings.)

➤ *Several preschool teachers said they made the paper owl bigger and used a larger paper bag for its tree home.*

It is not important that these creations look like owls. The placement of the eyes, beak, and wings reflect a young child's vision, and the child is just beginning to observe nature and express what she sees, understands, and imagines.

Each child needs an oval shape cut from brown construction paper for an owl body, two smaller brown ovals for wings, two small yellow or white circles for eyes, a black triangle for a beak, paste, and a black crayon or marker.

The Child-Designed Owl

If the children have the necessary skills, let them design, cut out, and assemble their own owls. These owls may be somewhat realistic or very imaginative. The purpose of this approach is to encourage the children's creativity and promote their independence.

➤ *A kindergarten teacher said she chose the child-designed owl so the children would use their imaginations and be creative.*

The girls and boys need sheets of brown, black, and yellow construction paper, scissors, paste, and black markers or crayons.

The Owl Model

The process of assembling pre-cut owl parts encourages the children to think about what a real owl has on its body as they make an owl with eyes, a beak, two tufts, two wings, legs, and feet with four toes. Although structured, it allows for individual expression in the placement of the body parts. No two owls ever look alike.

If you select this approach, you need to prepare materials in advance. Follow the What You Need, Getting Ready, and Making Owl Models sections that follow.

WHAT YOU NEED

For the whole group

❏ 1 large pair of scissors
❏ 1 tray

Optional
❏ 1 hole punch

For each child and yourself

❏ A 4" x 9" sheet of brown paper
❏ A 1" x 2" sheet of yellow paper, or 2 yellow peel-and-stick dots, or 2 hole reinforcements
❏ 1 black triangle (Pattern F on page 62)
❏ 1 black crayon or marker
❏ Paste or glue

Optional
❏ Several feathers

GETTING READY

Anytime Before the Activity

Use the patterns on page 62 to cut out one paper owl for each child and one for yourself. For each owl cut out:

- One owl body (Pattern B) out of brown paper.

- Two wings (Pattern E) out of brown paper.

- Two tufts (Pattern F) out of brown paper.

- One beak (Pattern F) out of black paper.

- Two eyes (Pattern G) out of yellow paper, or use peel-and-stick dots or paper reinforcements.

Optional
- Use a hole punch to cut out a hole in each yellow dot to represent the pupil of each owl eye.

Immediately Before the Activity

1. Spread newspapers on the tables. Place paste, one black crayon, one paper owl body, and two owl eyes at each child's work space.

2. Have the paper wings, beaks, and tufts nearby to distribute when the children are ready for them.

3. Place one tray with newspaper, paste, one black crayon, and paper owl parts in the area where you present the activity.

Owl Shapes

1. Gather the boys and girls in a circle on the floor, and spread a paper oval (owl body), triangle (beak), and circle (eye) on the floor.

2. Have the children identify the shapes.

3. Tell the youngsters they will use the shapes to make an owl.

4. Hold up the oval and say, "This can be the owl's head and body."

Making Owl Models

1. Have the children help you make a paper owl.

   a. Write your name on the owl body cutout, and turn it over to hide your name.

   b. Ask, "What do owls have on their faces?" *[Eyes, Beak]* Hold up the circle and ask, "What part of the owl looks like this?" *[Eye]* Stick on two eyes.

   c. Hold up the black triangle and ask, "What part of the owl can this be?" *[Beak]* Glue on the beak.

   d. Ask, "What else does our owl need?" *[Wings, Legs]* As the children name these parts, glue on the wings. Draw the legs and ask, "How many claws does the owl need on its feet?" *[Four]* Draw four claws on each foot.

   e. Ask, "What do some owls have on top of their head that looks like ears?" *[Feathers]* Glue two paper tufts or two real feathers on top of the owl's head.

   Optional
   Ask, "What do owls have all over their wings and bodies to keep them warm?" *[Feathers]* Glue a few feathers onto the owl's body.

2. Send the children to the tables to make their own owls.

   a. Have the children write their names on their owls. If they are unable to write their own names, write their names for them.

   b. Have the children turn the owls over to hide the names.

c. After the children put on the eyes, distribute the beaks, tufts, and wings.

d. Encourage the children to draw legs and feet with four claws.

Optional
Let the youngsters glue a few feathers onto their owls.

3. If the children glue on the wings in an outstretched position, help them fold the wings so that the owls can "fly" into the paper-bag tree holes during the activity More Owl Drama on page 55.

Creative Play

Encourage the children to play with their paper owls. They can "fly" them around the room or yard and pretend the owls are calling, "whoooo, whoooo."

Session 3
NESTS, EGGS, AND BABY OWLS

WHAT YOU NEED

For the whole group
❏ 1 pair of large scissors

For each child and yourself
❏ 1 paper owl
❏ A 1" white paper square
❏ 1 pencil
❏ 1 paper lunch bag

Optional
❏ A copy of "The Owl Finger Play" on page 60

GETTING READY

Anytime Before the Activity

1. Cut one hole (Pattern B on page 62) in each paper lunch bag to make tree homes. (See the drawing on this page.)

2. Write your name on a paper-bag tree and the children's names on their trees.

3. Cut out one white paper egg (Pattern J on page 63) for each child and yourself.

Immediately Before the Activity

Prepare for another owl drama.

- Place your paper-bag tree in the area where you present the drama. Have your paper owl looking out of the hole.

- Scatter small sticks on the ground near the tree.

MORE OWL DRAMA

1. Gather the children in a half circle in front of your paper-bag tree. Present a drama using your paper owl, paper-bag tree, and small sticks as props.

- The owl flies to the ground and picks up a stick with its claws. It carries the stick to its tree hole (the hole in paper-bag tree) and drops it in to start its nest.

- The owl finds another stick and places it in its nest.

- Then the owl folds its wings close to its body and moves into its nest.

- It sits alone, looking out of its tree-hole nest.

2. Distribute the children's owls and paper-bag tree homes.

3. If possible, take the children outside with their owls and paper bags to collect sticks for the nests.

4. Encourage the children to place only a few sticks in their paper-bag trees. The youngsters can pretend the owls are flying to the ground and picking up the sticks.

5. Back inside, have the children "fly" their owls into their nests. Have them create a paper-tree forest by grouping their paper-bag trees around the edge of a table.

6. While the children are sitting on the floor in front of the nests, darken the room and pretend that it is nighttime. Present "The Owl Finger Play" in front of the forest of owl homes.

The Owl Finger Play
(fold hands)
The owl sits alone in the hole of a tree,
(whisper)
And it is as quiet as quiet can be.
(make circles around eyes with fingers)
It is night and its eyes are round like this.
(turn head from side to side)
It looks all around; not a thing does it miss.
(make two fists)
Two mice climb onto a root of the tree,
(whisper)
And they are as quiet as quiet can be.
Says the wise old owl, "whooooo, whooooo."
(move fingers back and forth as if scurrying feet)
Off run the mice at the sound of the "whooooo."
(fold hands)
The owl sits alone in the hole of a tree,
(whisper)
And it is as quiet as quiet can be.

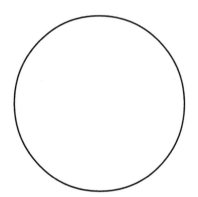

What is in the Nests?

1. Place a white paper egg in each nest. Tell the children to look in their nests and ask, "What did the mother owls leave in the nests?" *[Eggs]*

2. Pretend that the paper owl eggs hatch. Have the children draw faces and feet on the paper eggs, turning them into owlets. (See the drawing on this page.)

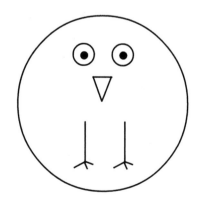

Role-Playing Baby Owls

1. Have the children pretend they are baby and parent owls.

2. The baby owls can snuggle up with their parents to get warm.

GOING FURTHER

Send the paper owls, paper-bag trees, and copies of "The Owl Finger Play" home with the children. Include a note asking the parents to do the finger play with their children.

Owl

OWL PATTERNS

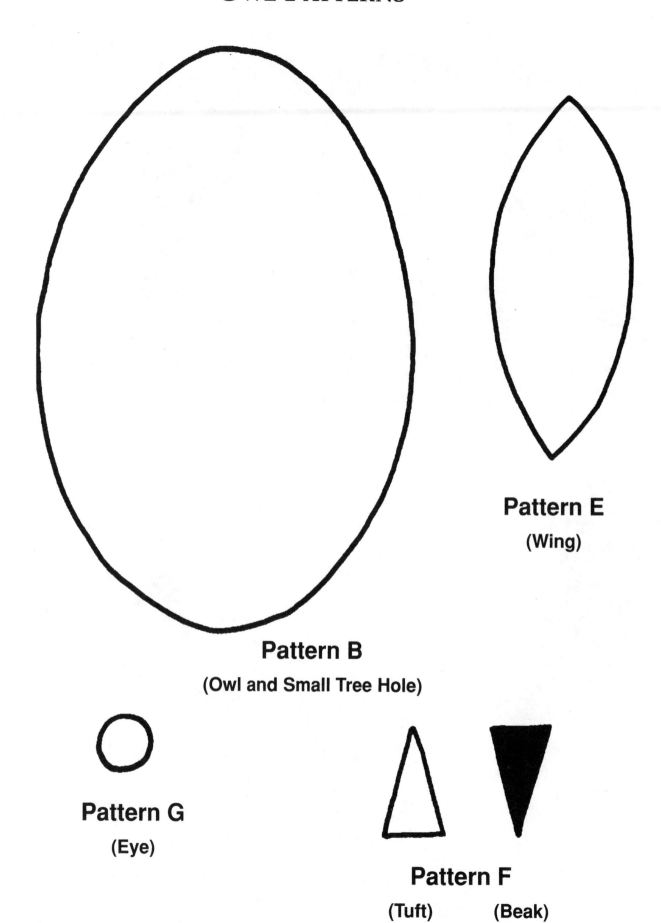

Pattern E

(Wing)

Pattern B

(Owl and Small Tree Hole)

Pattern G

(Eye)

Pattern F

(Tuft)   (Beak)

OWL PATTERNS

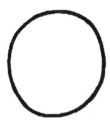

Pattern J

(Egg)

Pattern L

(Snake)

Pattern K

(Mouse)

Activity 6
MORE TREE HOMES

OVERVIEW

In this activity, the group learns that bears, raccoons, and owls move out of their tree-hole homes and other animals move in. From home the children bring toy rabbits, skunks, opossums, or any animals that could live in a tree hole.

During the More Tree Homes drama, the children suggest the most appropriate hole for each new animal. They take turns making the animals hop, climb, or fly into their new homes. The children create their own dramas as they play freely with the tree and the toy animals.

The boys and girls sort the toy animals by color, size, type, and by the number of legs on each animal. While looking at the Tree Homes poster, the children discuss the ways trees help animals and tell each other all the things they like about trees.

WHAT YOU NEED

For the group

- ❏ 1 large cardboard tree
- ❏ Several toy animals that could live in tree holes, such as rabbits, skunks, squirrels, opossums, birds, bees, or spiders.
- ❏ 1 large box or paper bag to hide the animals in
- ❏ 1 Tree Homes poster

GETTING READY

Several Days Before the Activity

1. For information about the variety of animals that live in trees, read Trees in the Background Information section on page 69.

2. Encourage the children to bring from home toy animals that could live in tree holes, such as the ones listed above.

3. Send home with the children a letter specifying the animals you need. Ask the parents to help their child think of animals that could live in trees.

Immediately Before the Activity

1. Place the cardboard tree in the area where you present the drama.

2. Hide the toy animals that could live in tree holes in the box. Put the box near the tree.

3. If the children bring animals that don't live in tree holes, find homes for those animals. For example, a toy dog or cat could live in the area where the children play house.

More Tree Homes Drama

1. Gather the children in a half circle around the cardboard tree. Present a drama showing how animals move out of their tree-hole homes and new animals move in. Ask questions that encourage the children to think about appropriate homes for the new animals.

- The bear family moves out of its tree hole and goes off into the woods looking for a new place to live. (Walk the bears out of their hole and away from the tree.)

- A rabbit hops (or a skunk wanders) over to the tree. Rabbits (or skunks) do not climb trees. Which hole do you think the rabbit (or skunk) would choose for a home? (Ask a child to place the animal in the bottom hole.)

- The raccoon climbs down the tree and goes off looking for a new home.

- The opossum (or squirrel) climbs up the tree. (Ask a child to find a hole that would make a safe and warm home for that animal.)

- The owl flies out of its hole and away to find a new home.

- A bird (or bee) flies to the tree. (Ask a child to fly the toy bird or bee into the smallest tree hole.)

2. Allow plenty of time for the children to create their own dramas as they play freely with the toy animals and the tree.

More Getting Warmer

1. Review how bears, raccoons, and owls get warmer.
   [snuggle together, go into sheltered places, bears and raccoons have fur, owls have feathers, raccoons wrap their furry tails around them]

2. Have the children look at the toy animals they brought from home and guess how those animals stay warm.

Sorting the Toy Animals

1. Have the children sort the toy animals in the same manner as in Sorting Bears on page 29.

2. In addition to sorting by color and size, they can sort by the type of animal, the number of legs on each animal, animals with wings and ones without wings, or by any other characteristics and attributes the children suggest.

The Tree Homes Poster

1. Show the children the Tree Homes poster and tell them the tree in the poster is no longer living. Ask, "What do you think the animals are doing in a dead tree?" *[they live there]*

2. Ask, "What animals do you see in the tree?" *[owl, squirrel, raccoon, woodpecker]*

3. Tell the youngsters that even when a tree is no longer living, it makes a good home for many animals.

Reflecting on Trees

1. Gather the children in a circle on the floor and ask, "What are some of the things you like about trees?" After the children express their ideas, you may want to tell them some of the things you like about trees.

2. Ask, "How do you think trees help animals?" After the children talk about the homes animals make in trees, ask questions that encourage the children to think about the food and nesting materials animals take from trees.

GOING FURTHER

If a child brings a toy monkey or toucan to class, bring in, and talk about, picture books about rain forests. Compare a rain forest and the animals that live in it with a nearby forest.

TREE HOMES

BACKGROUND INFORMATION

TREES

Animals of all sizes, from tiny insects to families of black bears, depend on trees for homes. Leaves, branches, bark, trunks, and roots attract specific animals. Aphids and caterpillars live on leaves. Beetles and ants are often found in crevices in the bark. Branches support bird and squirrel nests.

Sometimes tree branches break off, leaving holes in the trunk. The wood rots and insects chew the wood, increasing the size of the holes. Woodpeckers peck away at the wood, enlarging the holes for nests. Once the woodpeckers vacate their nests, rats, bats, or other small animals may occupy the space. As the sizes of the holes continue to increase, larger animals such as owls, squirrels, raccoons, and opossums move in.

Forest fires also produce holes by burning out the interior of trees. Heavy rains often wash soil away from tree roots, leaving large spaces under the roots. Holes at the base of trees and large spaces under roots provide homes for skunks, rabbits, and bears.

Strong winds occasionally blow trees down, creating logs. Hollow logs provide homes for skunks, rabbits, and bears. Ants, beetles, pill bugs, slugs, millipedes, centipedes, worms, and salamanders make their homes *under* logs.

A single old tree in the forest can support many more kinds of animals than the young trees surrounding it. In fact, many animals cannot survive in areas where there are no old trees for them to use as homes.

Protection, Shelter, and Food in Trees

Animals depend on trees for protection from other animals and for shelter from cold, heat, and rain. Cats climb trees to escape dogs. A hunting owl may not see a robin's nest hidden among leaves. A raccoon family sleeping in a tree hole usually stays warm and dry in stormy weather.

Animals of all sizes depend on trees for food. Leaves, sap, fruits, nuts, seeds, bark, and nectar nourish a variety of animals. Caterpillars and deer eat the leaves. Mice and bears feed on the nuts, seeds, and fruit. Butterflies sip the nectar. Other animals survive by eating the animals that live in trees. Owls eat squirrels, and raccoons eat birds and bird eggs.

BEARS

Black Bears

Black bears are a type of bear and are not always black; they can be dark brown, cinnamon, blue-black, or white with buff markings. They are smaller and much less aggressive than the brown or grizzly bear.

Food

Black bears spend much of their time searching for food. They have huge appetites, especially in the fall when they are getting fat in preparation for their long winter sleep. They eat a variety of small animals, including grasshoppers, ants, bees, small mammals, and fish. They also eat grasses, berries, fruits, nuts, acorns, and honey. Sometimes they eat young deer and porcupines. Occasionally black bears raid garbage cans and kill farm animals.

Homes and Young

Black bears are solitary animals, except during the mating season when the male and female spend a short time together. The bears breed in June and then go their separate ways. The male bear has no further role in parenting.

In the late summer or fall, the female bear makes a den in a hollow tree hole, log, or cave; under tree roots; or in a hole in the ground. She sleeps deeply during the winter and, in January or February, gives birth to two or three cubs. They are blind and toothless, have little hair, and are about the size of a kitten. The cubs nurse and snuggle up to their mother for warmth during the cold winter months. In the spring, they follow their mother out of the den and begin to explore the world. The mother bear teaches her playful cubs how to climb trees and hunt for food. She fiercely protects them from any danger. The cubs stay with their mother for at least six months, often up to two years.

Enemies

Black bears have well-developed senses of smell and hearing. They are good tree climbers, scurrying up trees when threatened. Black bears have several enemies. Old or sick bears are often killed by mountain lions, and sleeping bears are sometimes killed by wolves. Male bears kill young bears that are not protected by their mothers. Humans threaten the survival of black bears by cutting down the forests in which they live.

RACCOONS

Homes and Young

A female raccoon and her family of young raccoons (kits) inhabit many tree holes during different times of the year. In the spring, the mother raccoon finds a well-protected hole, usually high in a tree. Any loose rotted wood already in the hole makes a soft nest for her young. Raccoons have two to seven babies that are about three inches long and covered with grey fuzz. They are born with masks on their faces but no rings on their tails. At birth, the kits can neither see nor hear.

When the young are about eight weeks old, the mother often moves them to a hole at the base of a tree that is near water. By midsummer, the kits are old enough to leave their nest to hunt with their mother. As they look for food in the forest, they bed down in different tree holes or hollow logs along the way. In the late fall, the family usually moves into one tree hole for the winter months, sharing their body warmth to survive the cold weather. By spring the kits leave their mother. The young females find holes high in trees to begin raising their own families.

A female raccoon is an excellent mother. She fiercely protects her young against predators, such as dogs, owls, foxes, bobcats, and skunks. If her nest is disturbed, she moves her young to a new one. She carries her kits by the loose fur on their necks, like cats carry their young. A mother raccoon will even raise orphaned raccoons as members of her own family.

Food

Raccoons eat almost anything. Their diet includes earthworms, insect larvae, bird and turtle eggs, grasshoppers, mice, and shrews. At ponds and streams, they eat fish, frogs, tadpoles, and crayfish. They also eat corn, fruits, berries, nuts, acorns, and mushrooms. They eat animals that have been killed by cars and hunters. They even climb trees to pick and eat the fruit. Raccoons often visit houses to devour cat food and steal from garbage cans.

Intelligence

Raccoons are intelligent animals with good memories and well-developed senses of hearing, vision, smell, and touch. Their adaptability helps them to survive when cities and farmland replace large areas of their forest home.

OWLS

Most owls sleep in tree holes or on branches where they are well hidden by the leaves. Many owls lay their eggs and raise their young in tree holes. They find much of their food around or under trees.

Many different kinds of owls exist, varying in color as well as size. The smallest are the size of sparrows. The largest measure five feet across from wing tip to wing tip. There is no difference in coloring between male and female owls. However, female owls are usually larger than males.

All owls have large ears and eyes, curved beaks, and four toes on each foot. Each toe has a sharp curved claw, called a talon. Owl talons work like hooks to stab and hold a captured animal. The sharp beak is used to tear food that is too large to swallow whole. The large eyes help owls to see better at night, when most owls hunt. Owls have huge openings for ears hidden under head feathers. Large eyes and ears provide owls with excellent senses of sight and hearing, but owls have a very poor sense of smell.

Homes and Young

Owls build simple nests, if any at all. At most, they pick up a few sticks to put in a protected place, such as a tree hole. Sometimes they use abandoned squirrel, woodpecker, hawk, or crow nests.

Usually both parent owls help to take care of the young. The mother owl usually lays one to six round white eggs. The father brings food to the nesting female and occasionally shares the job of sitting on the eggs. When the owlets (or chicks) first hatch, they are weak and helpless with closed eyes. Soon they are covered with fluffy white down. Both parents bring food to the young and protect them from danger. The mother owl teaches the owlets to fly and hunt for food. The young stay with their parents until they are about three months old.

Food

Owls eat a variety of animals. They help farmers by eating large numbers of rodents and insects that can become pests. Large owls eat snakes, rabbits, squirrels, skunks, rats, and mice. Small owls eat crickets, beetles, moths, grasshoppers, and other insects. They also eat earthworms, snails, and spiders. Many owls eat birds, and some eat fish and frogs. When an owl eats, it often swallows the animal whole, including its fur and bones. Hours later, it coughs up balls of fur and bones. These balls are called owl pellets.

Enemies

Owls have only a few enemies, including hawks, eagles, and humans. Sometimes large owls kill smaller owls. Weasels, martens, and large snakes climb trees to take eggs and owlets from owl nests. Owls can die from pesticides and insecticides. The owls eat the poisoned rodents and insects, and die. Cutting down forests also endangers the survival of some species of owls. For example, the spotted owl is adapted for living in old growth forests and is on the endangered species list because of loss of habitat.

Assessment Suggestions

Selected Student Outcomes

1. Students gain familiarity with a tree's structure, and its role as a home to animals as they observe living trees and the animals that live on them.

2. Students demonstrate their knowledge about animal homes as they participate in role plays of different animals that live in tree holes.

3. Students describe the behaviors that help animals stay warm, feed, protect themselves, and raise their young in trees.

4. Students develop the concept of measurement through size comparisons. They use size as well as other attributes to sort and classify toy animals and other objects.

Built-In Assessment Activities

Getting to Know Trees

In Activity 1, A Tree and Its Holes, students observe living trees with live animals. They later compare the tree to the cardboard tree they construct. The teacher observes the children's understanding of tree parts as students describe and compare the structures on both trees. She also notes students ability to observe and describe animals living on trees. (Outcomes 1, 4)

A Tree Home for Bears

In Activity 2, Black Bears, students learn that black bears can use a large hole in a tree to keep warm and to raise their cubs. Children watch a drama about bears and their young, and pretend that they are bears who keep warm in a tree. The role plays and dramas allow students to demonstrate their understanding of a bear's need for a tree-hole home. The teacher can observe how students communicate these concepts to friends and family when activities are repeated at home and at school. (Outcomes 2, 3)

Sorting Bears

In Session 2, Activity 2, students sort toy bears by color and size as well as other attributes (features) they observe on their bears. The More Sorts has children describe attributes and sort nuts, leaves, wooden objects, and fruit according to those attributes. (Outcome 4)

Keeping Warm

In Activity 3, Getting Warmer, children learn that people wear clothes, move around, and sip warm drinks to keep warm. The children compare how bears and humans keep warm. Teachers can observe students' insights and logical thinking as they watch the activities and listen to responses in discussions. (Outcomes 2, 3)

Making a Model

In Activity 5, Owls, children watch a short drama about a pair of owls who live in a tree. They make a model of an owl and build a paper bag nest. The teacher can observe the model of the owl and nest, and note how it is used in dramas and role plays. The teacher can look for descriptive language and new vocabulary used by the children as well as dramatics that describe the various behaviors of owls. (Outcomes 2, 3)

Other Animals That Live in Trees

In Activity 6, More Tree Homes, children bring specific toy animals to school that could live in trees. As an assessment opportunity, ask the children to think of another animal that could live in trees and to bring in a toy or picture of that animal. The children can present the animal and describe or act out where the animal would live. The teacher can observe the richness of the children's explanations as compared to their earlier responses to the bear, raccoon, and owl experiences. (Outcomes 1, 2, 3)

Additional Assessment Ideas

Writing About Tree Homes

Have your students write or dictate stories about their owl's, raccoon's, or toy bear's life in a tree. (Outcome 3)

Trees through the Seasons

Keep the cardboard tree in the classroom during the whole school year and change the tree (different colored leaves, fewer or more leaves, blossoms, fruit) to match the different seasons. Continue to observe the living tree outdoors. Introduce new animals and have children come up with new stories and role plays to act out. (Outcomes 1, 2, 3)

RESOURCE BOOKS

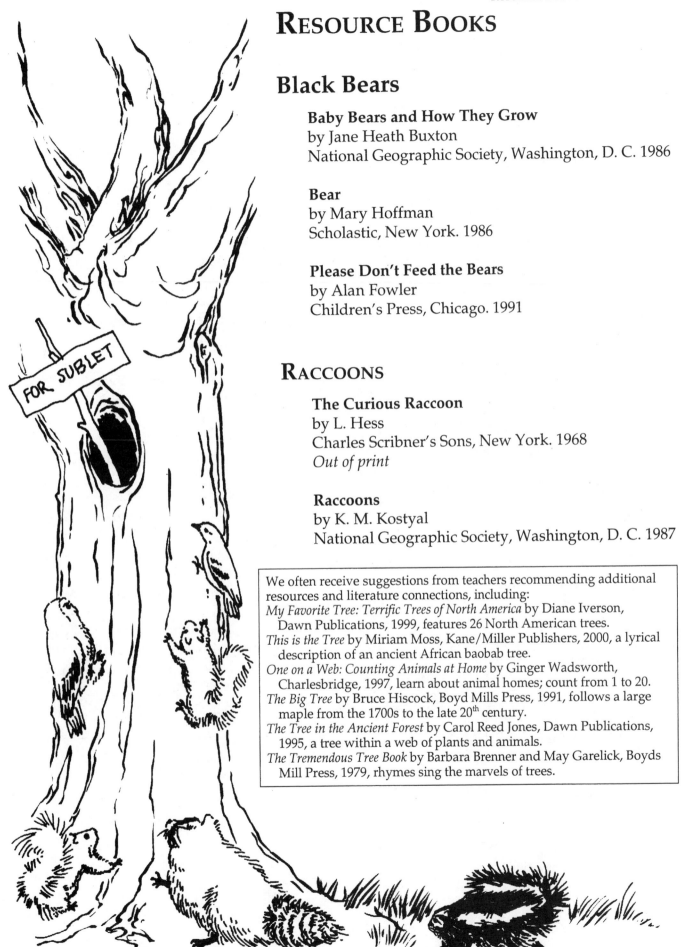

Black Bears

Baby Bears and How They Grow
by Jane Heath Buxton
National Geographic Society, Washington, D. C. 1986

Bear
by Mary Hoffman
Scholastic, New York. 1986

Please Don't Feed the Bears
by Alan Fowler
Children's Press, Chicago. 1991

RACCOONS

The Curious Raccoon
by L. Hess
Charles Scribner's Sons, New York. 1968
Out of print

Raccoons
by K. M. Kostyal
National Geographic Society, Washington, D. C. 1987

We often receive suggestions from teachers recommending additional resources and literature connections, including:
My Favorite Tree: Terrific Trees of North America by Diane Iverson, Dawn Publications, 1999, features 26 North American trees.
This is the Tree by Miriam Moss, Kane/Miller Publishers, 2000, a lyrical description of an ancient African baobab tree.
One on a Web: Counting Animals at Home by Ginger Wadsworth, Charlesbridge, 1997, learn about animal homes; count from 1 to 20.
The Big Tree by Bruce Hiscock, Boyd Mills Press, 1991, follows a large maple from the 1700s to the late 20th century.
The Tree in the Ancient Forest by Carol Reed Jones, Dawn Publications, 1995, a tree within a web of plants and animals.
The Tremendous Tree Book by Barbara Brenner and May Garelick, Boyds Mill Press, 1979, rhymes sing the marvels of trees.

Owls

About Owls
by May Garelick
Four Winds Press, New York. 1975
Out of print

The Mother Owl
by Edith T. Hurd
Little, Brown & Co., Boston. 1974
Out of print

Owls
Zoobooks, Vol. 1, No. 6 (March 1985)
Wildlife Education, San Diego,
California

See How They Grow
photos by Kim Taylor
Doring Kindersley, New York. 1992

More Tree Homes

Animals That Live in Trees
by J.R. McCauley
National Geographic Society,
Washington, D.C. 1986

Be a Friend to Trees
by Patricia Lauber
Lets-Read-And-Find-Out Science
HarperCollins, New York. 1994

The Squirrel in the Trees
by Jennifer Coldrey
Oxford Scientific Films
(Animal Habitats)
Gareth Stevens, Milwaukee,
Wisconsin. 1986

The Tree A First Discovery Book
by Gallimard Jeunesse and
Pascale de Bourgoing
Illustrated by Christian Broutin
Scholastic Inc., New York. 1992
Grades: Preschool–2

The life of a chestnut tree is
chronicled through the seasons as it
sprouts from a seed, blossoms,
grows, sheds leaves, and drops new
chestnuts that will one day become
trees themselves. There are de-
scriptions of different types of trees,
how to recognize them, and beautiful plastic overlays that illustrate
the parts of a chestnut tree and the
life it contains.

RESOURCE MATERIALS ────────────

Trees

Full Option Science System (FOSS)
Lawrence Hall of Science
University of California
Berkeley, CA 94720
(510) 642-8941
   (To order, call Delta Education at 1-800-258-1302.)

LITERATURE CONNECTIONS

A Tree and Its Holes

Grandmother Oak
by Rosi Dagit
Roberts Rinehart, Boulder, Colo. 1996
Grades: Preschool–3

The story of a 200-year-old giant Californian oak recounts the events in its long life and the life that happened in and around it.

Hello, Tree
by Joanne Ryder
Lodestar Books, New York. 1991
Grades: K–3

This story encourages an appreciation for the beauty, growth, shade, sounds, smells, and textures of a tree and for the animals seen in the tree.

Look at Trees
by Rena Kirkpatrick
Raintree Children's Books,
Milwaukee. 1978
Grades: Preschool–1

This easy-to-read text introduces, with illustrations and pictures, various types of trees.

The Mighty Tree
by Dick Gackenbach
Voyager Books, Harcourt Brace & Co.,
New York. 1996
Grades: Preschool–2

Three seeds grow into three beautiful trees, each of which serves important purposes. One tree provides paper, cardboard, books, and shopping bags; another becomes a holiday tree for a city; and the third remains in the woods as a home and shelter for animals.

My House: A Pop-Up Book
by Noelle Carter
Viking Penguin, New York. 1991
Grades: Preschool–1

This brightly illustrated book features lift-the-flap, pop-up surprises showing the habitats and homes where different animals live. It includes a tree home for a squirrel as well as a home for a young boy and his family.

Night Gliders
by Joanne Ryder
Roberts Rinehart, Boulder, Colo. 1997
Grades: Preschool–3

Wonderful illustrations complement the poetic story of a flying squirrel.

Night Tree
by Eve Bunting
Harcourt Brace Jovanovich,
San Diego. 1991
Grades: Preschool–3

Each Christmas a family goes to a nearby forest to decorate a tree with food for the animals.

Our Very Own Tree
by Lawrence F. Lowery
Encyclopaedia Britannica
Educational Corp., Chicago. 1993
Grades: K–3

Two friends have a special tree they often visit. Through the discoveries of these two little girls, children have a wonderful opportunity to learn about trees and the animals that live in them. This 12" x 18" book is beautifully illustrated and has a built-in stand.
(To order, call Delta Education at 1-800-258-1302; order number 42-021-6457)

Literature Connections

A Tree is Nice
by Janice Udry
Harper & Row, New York. 1956
Grades: Preschool–1
Simple text and colorful illustrations express the many joys children find in trees.

Trees
by Harry Behn
Henry Holt and Company, N.Y. 1992
Grades: Preschool–2
This beautifully illustrated poem celebrates the importance of trees.

Willy and the Cardboard Boxes
by Lizi Boyd
Viking, A Division of Penguin Books, New York, 1991
Grades: Preschool–1
With the help of his imagination and a lot of empty computer boxes at his father's office, Willy flies into a colorful world where the boxes become among many things an airplane, a tunnel, a horse, and a fire engine. Just as the children use cardboard boxes to make the tree in this guide, they can also use additional boxes to craft things from their imaginations just like Willy!

Black Bears

The Bear & The Fly
by Paula Winter
Crown Publishers, New York. 1976
Grades: Preschool–2
This wordless book has delightful illustrations of a family of three bears whose dinner is interrupted by a fly. As Papa Bear tries to catch the fly, there are disastrous results. This book is wonderful for language development as the children can tell their version of the story to accompany the pictures.

Black Bear Baby
by Bernice Freschet
G. P. Putnam's Sons, New York. 1981
Out of print
Grades: Preschool–2
This story about Black Bear Baby and his sister realistically describes the early life of Black Bear cubs.

Goldilocks and the Three Bears
retold and illustrated by Jan Brett
Dodd, Mead & Company, N.Y. 1987
Grades: Preschool–2
This classic tale introduces a consistent and predictable size comparison as Goldilocks encounters the three bowls of porridge, the three chairs, the three beds, and finally, the three bears themselves. The book has gorgeous illustrations that show a system of interacting plants and animals including caterpillars changing into butterflies, and many varieties of seeds, leaves, bird eggs, and forest scenes.

Two Little Bears

by Ylla

Harper & Row, New York. 1954

Out of print

Grades: Preschool–2

The adventures of two lost bear cubs come to an end when their mother finds them. Beautiful large photographs capture the cubs in delightful poses.

Winnie-The-Pooh

by A.A. Milne;

illustrations by Ernest H. Shepard

E.P. Dutton, New York. 1926

Dell Publishing, New York. 1954

Grades: All Ages

This well-loved classic contains chapter after delightful chapter of the adventures of Christopher Robin, Pooh, and their animal friends—most of whom live in tree homes. Relevant chapters include one in which Pooh visits Piglet who lives in the bottom of a beech tree (Chapter 3) and one in which Pooh becomes struck trying to leave rabbit's home after eating an entire pot of honey (Chapter 2). This book works well read aloud to younger children.

Getting Warmer

The Day The Sun Danced

by Edith T. Hurd

Harper & Row, New York. 1965

Grades: K–3

During the darkness and cold of winter, the rabbit goes to the bear, the fox, and the deer to tell them that something is going to happen. Beautiful woodcuts contrast the bleakness of winter and the brilliant colors of spring.

Raccoons

Baby Raccoon

by Beth Spanjian

Longmeadow Press,

Stamford, Conn. 1988

Grades: Preschool–1

Baby Raccoon along with his mother, sisters, and brothers leave their tree home nest for an adventurous search for food on a beautiful, moonlit summer night.

Raccoons and Ripe Corn

by Jim Arnosky

Lothrop, Lee and Shepard Books,

New York. 1987

Grades: Preschool–3

Mother raccoon and her kits feast on corn all night long under a full moon. The large color illustrations show the raccoons in delightfully realistic poses.

Owls

Good-Night, Owl!

by Pat Hutchins

Macmillan Publishing Co., N.Y. 1972

Grades: Preschool–2

Owl is kept awake during the day by all the noisy animals that live in the tree near him. Night comes and the situation changes.

Owl At Home

by Arnold Lobel

Scholastic Book Services, N.Y. 1975

Grades: Preschool–2

These five easy-to-read stories feature Owl, whose many delightful adventures range from discovering that his knees are the bumps in his bed to preparing tear-water tea.

Literature Connections

Owl Babies

by Martin Waddell;
illustrated by Patrick Benson.
Candlewick Press,
Cambridge, Mass. 1992
Grades: Preschool–1

Three baby owls wake up one night in their tree home and find their mother gone. They fret and worry until finally she comes back safely to the nest. Beautifully illustrated, this story shares the strong tie between mother and babies so familiar to young children.

Owl Lake

by Keizaburo Tejima
Philomel Books, N.Y. 1982
Out of print
Grades: Preschool–2

Bold woodcuts illustrate the story of a father owl who flies across a lake in the moonlight searching for silver fish to feed his hungry family.

Owl Moon

by Jane Yolen
Philomel Books, New York. 1987
Grades: Preschool–2

Large watercolor illustrations enhance this story about a little girl and her father who go into the woods on a moonlit night in search of a Great Horned Owl. The child learns from her father that you need to be quiet, brave, and hopeful when you go looking for owls.

Whoo-oo Is It?

by Megan McDonald
Orchard Books, Franklin Watts,
New York. 1992
Grades: Preschool–1

Mother Owl hears a noise in the night and finally finds out what is making the mysterious sound.

➤ *You may wish to examine the literature listings in these GEMS teacher's guides in the GEMS handbook* Once Upon A GEMS Guide: Connecting Young People's Literature to Great Explorations in Math and Science:

Animal Defenses
Ant Homes Under the Ground
Buzzing A Hive
Eggs Eggs Everywhere
Hide A Butterfly
Penguins and Their Young
Terrarium Habitats

Also, please see the age-appropriate listings in the science themes—especially Systems & Interactions—as well as the math strands sections in the handbook.

In addition, the above teacher's guides include exciting activities that would make excellent accompaniments to Tree Homes.

SUMMARY OUTLINES

ACTIVITY 1: A TREE AND ITS HOLES

Session 1: The Living Tree

Visiting a Living Tree
1. Gather group around tree. Hold hands around trunk if possible, and move in circle.
2. Ask why a tree needs roots. [*to bring food/water from soil, help tree stand*] Have children identify parts of tree.
3. Children close eyes, describe feel/smell of bark. Listen for sounds of tree. Open eyes and describe bark.
4. Why does a tree need bark [*for protection*]
5. Children compare bark to skin on their hands.
6. Children describe tree colors, discuss how leaves help trees.
7. Look with children for small holes in tree and any small animals.
8. Have children pretend to be small animals they see on tree.

Observing Real Branches
1. Spread branches on table for children to observe.
2. Ask questions to encourage close observation.

Session 2: The Cardboard Tree

Making the Cardboard Tree
1. Show materials and explain making a cardboard tree.
2. Children paint boxes and paper rolls brown.
3. When dry, glue or fasten boxes together.
4. Children insert branches into small holes.

Attaching Leaves
1. If using paper leaves, demonstrate cutting/tearing corners.
2. Show how to tape real or paper leaves to tree.

Comparing the Real and Cardboard Tree
1. Encourage discussion of real tree.
2. Have children identify parts of cardboard tree.
3. Ask about holes and how big holes in trees might be made.

Tree Hole Sizes
1. Gather children in front of cardboard tree.
2. Children compare size of holes.
3. Children match ovals with appropriate holes.

ACTIVITY 2: BLACK BEARS

Session 1: Bear Drama and Role Playing

1. Set up for drama: cardboard tree, toy bears, acorns/nuts/berries.
2. Present bear drama as in guide.
   Optional: Add more toy bears from home to drama.

Session 2: Sorting Bears

1. Children, in circle, introduce their bears.
2. Ask for observations, encourage with questions.
3. Start sorting by color.
4. As child suggests color, place bear of that color inside circle.
5. Continue until all colors named and all bears sorted.
6. Ask counting/comparison questions.
7. Depending on interest/ability sort in a new way, such as size.
8. Discuss and agree on words to describe sizes.
9. Go around circle, with bears placed according to size.
10. Ask counting/comparison questions.

ACTIVITY 3: GETTING WARMER

What Clothes Keep You Warm?

1. Gather children in circle. Review how bears get warm.
2. Ask, "What can you use to keep you warm?"
3. As items suggested, take out of box and put in circle.
4. Allow plenty of time for ideas.
5. You could quickly draw items named that are not in box.
6. Count all the items and put back in box.

Snuggling
1. "What can you snuggle under to get warm?" [*blankets*]
2. Children snuggle under blankets.
3. Children put on coats and pretend they are little bears.
4. Children snuggle together to get even warmer.

Being Active
1. Gather children in circle.
2. "Are you warmer when you stand still or jump up and down?"
3. Children jump to find out.
4. "How else can you move to get warmer?"

Sun Activity (in sunlight in room or outside)
1. Children find a sunny place and put their hands in the sunlight.
2. Children find an area not in the sun and compare.
3. Animals and plants get warmer in the sun.

Friction
1. Rub your hands together. Children do the same.
2. "What happens?" [*hands get warmer*]
3. "What else can you rub to get warmer?" [*arms, legs*]

ACTIVITY 4: RACCOONS

Session 1: Getting to Know Raccoons

Introducing the Raccoon
1. "I'm thinking of animal with fur, a black mask, stripes on tail ... "
2. Show toy/puppet raccoon.
3. Exchange experiences.

The Raccoon Drama
Tell story and act out drama as in guide.

The Raccoon Poster

1. Display poster to group, have children point to features.
2. Why does raccoon have mask? Accept all ideas. *[mask makes eyes harder to see]*
3. Children count legs and toes. How is your foot like a raccoon's?
4. Children count stripes on tail. Is tail bigger/smaller than body?

Raccoon Creative Play

1. Children pretend to be raccoons keeping warm, with sweaters, towels, etc., as "tails."
2. Children make raccoon masks and tails, and crawl into "tree homes."

Session 2: Raccoon Snacks

1. Partially darken room, pretend it's late at night.
2. At snack time, give each child lunch bag of raccoon snacks.
3. Encourage children to feel inside bag and guess what items are.

Session 3: Making Paper-Bag Raccoons

Making Raccoon Puppets

1. Children help you make a paper bag raccoon.
2. Children make their own.
3. Children (or you) write names on their raccoons.

Creative Play

Allow plenty of free time for children to play with their puppets.

ACTIVITY 5: OWLS

Session 1: Getting to Know Owls

The Owl Poster

1. Display poster. "What bird is this?" [*owl*]
2. Child finds eyes. How do big eyes help owls?
3. Explain that owls can turn their heads all the way around.
4. Children find nostrils, wings, claws, and count claws.

Real Feathers

1. What does owl have all over that is soft? [*feathers*]
2. Pass feathers around. How do feathers help owls? [*Warmth*]
3. Explain that tufts are feathers; ears are at side of head.

Comparisons

1. Gather children and "fly" mother and father owl to them.
2. Ask which is bigger. Explain that mother owls are bigger.
3. Ask which is mother owl.
4. Ask child to find tree hole for mother owl.

The Owl Drama

1. Darken room and pretend it's night.
2. Present drama as in guide.
3. Encourage children to play creatively with tree/drama animals.
4. Have books with owl pictures available.

Session 2: Making Paper Owls

Owl Shapes
1. Spread paper owl body, beak, eye on floor.
2. Have children identify shapes.
3. They will use shapes to make an owl.
4. Hold up oval: "This can be the owl's head and body."

Making Owl Models
1. Have the children help you make paper owl as in guide.
2. Children make their own paper owls.
3. Children (or you) write names on owls, then turn over.
4. After eyes are on, give out beaks, tufts, wings.
5. Encourage drawing legs and feet with four claws.
6. Help children fold wings as needed.
7. Encourage creative play.

Session 3: Nests, Eggs, and Baby Owls

More Owl Drama
1. Present drama of owl making nest as in guide.
2. Hand out children's owls and paper-bag tree homes.
3. If possible, go outside so they can find sticks.
4. Children place **a few** sticks in nests.
5. Inside, children fly "owls" to nests.
6. Darken room and present the "Owl Finger Play."

What is in the Nests?
1. Put white paper egg in each nest.
2. What did the mother owl leave there? [*eggs*]
3. Pretend eggs hatch. Children draw on paper eggs to turn them into owlets.
4. Children role-play baby and parent owls.

ACTIVITY 6: MORE TREE HOMES

More Tree Homes Drama
1. Present drama as in guide.
2. Children create their own tree home dramas.

More Getting Warmer
1. Review how bears, raccoons, owls get warmer.
2. How do animals represented by toy animals stay warm?

Sorting the Toy Animals
1. Children sort toy animals as in Sorting Bears activity.
2. Can also sort by type of animal, number of legs, etc.

The Tree Homes Poster
1. Display poster.
2. The tree is no longer living, what are animals doing in it? [*they live there*]
3. What animals do you see in the tree?

Reflecting on Trees
1. "What are some things you like about trees?"
2. "How do you think trees help animals?"

PARTS OF A TREE

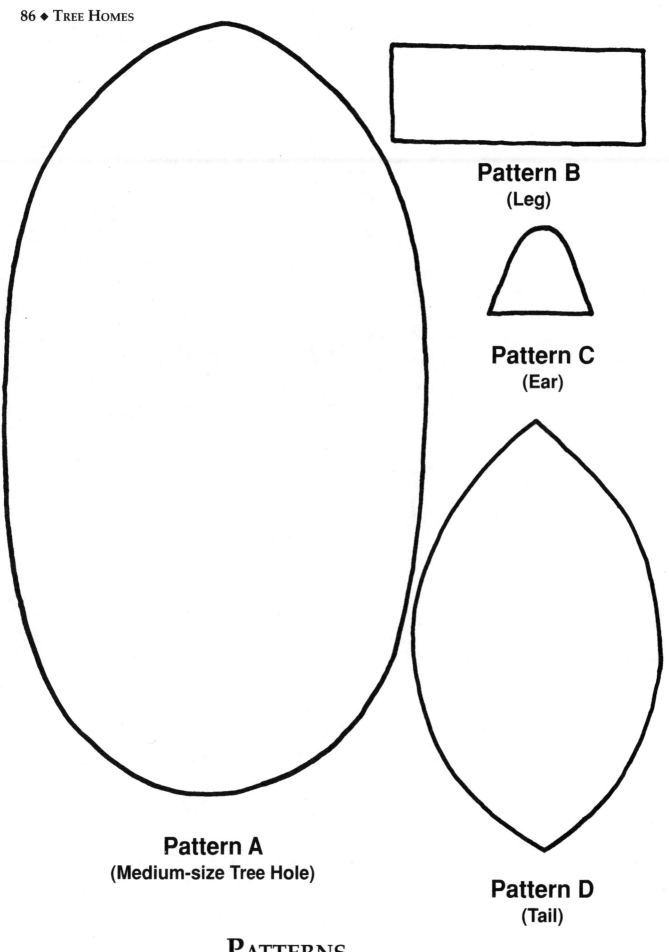

Pattern B
(Leg)

Pattern C
(Ear)

Pattern A
(Medium-size Tree Hole)

Pattern D
(Tail)

Patterns

OWL PATTERNS

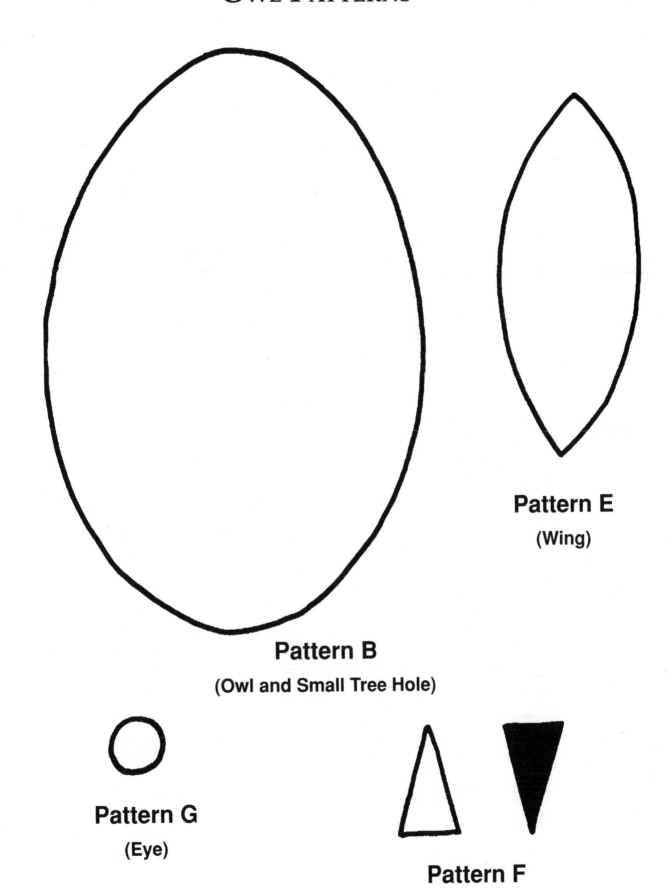

Pattern E

(Wing)

Pattern B

(Owl and Small Tree Hole)

Pattern G

(Eye)

Pattern F

(Tuft)   (Beak)

OWL PATTERNS

Pattern J

(Egg)

Pattern L

(Snake)

Pattern K

(Mouse)